GIDEON

GOD'S MIGHTY MAN OF VALOR

LIVING WITH GOD THROUGH
A TRUSTING FAITH

"I read this book in one day and didn't want it to end and wished I was reading it with a group! Well done! In *Gideon, God's Man of Mighty Valor*, Dr. Hartman weaves what we know of Gideon from the Bible with well-researched historical accuracy.

"The detailed research clearly benefits the reader by painting Gideon in full color against the backdrop of his community, his family, and his culture. In addition, the narrative is written in amazingly clear language. The story of Gideon, as told, shows us that while prayer is a crucial component of our faith how it is essential to be aware of God's answers to our prayers. His response is there if we are open to recognizing His presence and are patient in understanding His answers.

"Valor doesn't just mean courage in physical battle; Dr. Hartman shows us through Gideon that it also means having the personal strength and courage when we kneel before God and ask for guidance and stand with arms outstretched to give praise. The quiet voice of Gideon's faith resides in every page of this book!"

—**BONNIE SMITH**, RN, BSN, MFA

"Find out how Gideon, overlooked by society because he didn't come from the right part of town, helped God save the Israelites. Discover why Gideon's overwhelming desire to please God and his humble background made him the perfect person for God to raise up as a hero.

"Dr. Hartman takes the story of Gideon and explains it in a way that makes it extraordinarily relevant for us in the 21st century. With a mix of creative storytelling and biblical scholarship, Dr. Hartman gives his readers a chance to think deeply about their own lives."

—**STEVEN HARRIS**, host, *Kingdom of God Entrepreneur Show*

"*Gideon, God's Mighty Man of Valor* is a remarkable book, immersed in a moment in history when one man refused to succumb to his fears by trusting God. Gideon is a seemingly insignificant man of his tribe; his great faith in the Lord thrusts him forward to save the Israelites from the hands of the Midianites. Dr. Hartman writes with descriptive detail and vividness, which transports us to Gideon's world, cheering him on. A great lesson in the value of faith."

—CLAUDIA PARKER, author

"After I finished *Gideon, God's Mighty Man of Valor*, my overall reaction was wow! This book is a timeless tale of courage and humility, as relevant today as 3,000 years ago. A master at blending biblical insight and historical context with compelling storytelling, Dr. Hartman reveals nuances shedding new light on Gideon, the man while challenging the reader to examine their faith.

"Dr. Hartman truly brought this story to life in a way I have never seen before. Even though I knew how the story ends like most readers, the journey through different times in history is eye-opening. I love how the story reminds us of the history that led to this important point in time—Joseph, Abraham, etc.

"The most striking thing about Gideon, the man for me, was his prayer life and how his strength came from a consistent daily prayer practice that enabled him to trust and heed God's calling. The story is much like the present day, making this book a commentary on America in 2022."

—JULIE WYCKOFF, business owner, M.ED

"Gideon, God's Mighty Man of Valor presents an in-depth and compelling historical narrative that brings Gideon to life in a personal way. Whether you are familiar with Gideon or not, Dr. Hartman invites the reader to reflect on their own life and how they acknowledge and answer God's calling. With compelling and thought-provoking faith questions, you will be challenged like Gideon as you are guided to the ultimate Judge, Jesus Christ!"

—RODNEY TILLOTSON, business owner

"Dr. Hartman is a wise man with a warm heart."

—DR. HEATHER MURRAY ELKINS, author of *Holy Stuff of Life*

"Dr. Hartman is a holistic visionary and master-detail examiner."

—DAN CASTELLANO, UX Evangelist

GIDEON

GOD'S MIGHTY MAN OF VALOR

LIVING WITH GOD THROUGH A TRUSTING FAITH

DR. BRUCE L. HARTMAN

HIGH BRIDGE BOOKS
HOUSTON

Gideon, God's Mighty Man of Valor
by Dr. Bruce L. Hartman

Printed in the United States of America
ISBN: 978-1-954943-36-0

High Bridge Books titles may be purchased in bulk for educational, business, fundraising, or sales promotional use. For information, please contact High Bridge Books via www.HighBridge-Books.com/contact.

Published in Houston, Texas by High Bridge Books

Contents

Preamble

For a long time, I have known about Gideon and his story in the book of Judges. I had gathered much of what I previously knew from early Sunday school lessons and my theological studies at Drew University. For me, it was always a story about how God compels us to strengthen our faith.

The Gideon story is also a simple reminder to trust God in all things and not turn away from God during the inevitable trials of life.

Gideon's story helps us face our foes without being paralyzed by fear. We will always have fear. But fear is conquered by trusting God with a persistent and patient faith. The courage we receive through our faith allows us to move forward and past fear.

As I started my research for the book, I discovered hidden treasures in Gideon's story. I began to see a universal tale about faith in the one true God and the persistent struggle between good and evil. As I studied the four pages of the Gideon story tucked away in the book of Judges, I found it far deeper than what I learned in Sunday school, my previous readings, or studies of the Bible.

While conducting research for the book, I discovered a universal connection between Gideon's story and the whole Bible. I began to realize that to fully explain all of the events in Gideon's story, I also had to include a deeper history of biblical events, like the adventures of Moses and the origin of the twelve tribes of the Israelites. The three chapters in the book of Judges (chapters 6–8, just four pages) are filled with subtle messages and history.

These subtleties can easily be missed without the advantage of historical knowledge of life from three thousand years ago and knowledge of ancient Hebrew. For instance, I discovered the names used in this story have specific meanings and give further insight into the account. These subtleties reveal that the Gideon story is also deeply connected to a significant span of human history, from Abraham to the twenty-first century.

Here is an example of what I mean. As I read one of the early verses in the story, I found Gideon threshing wheat in a winepress, which seemed odd and aroused my curiosity.

As a theological student of the Bible, I was taught to look deeper at these inconsistencies. Gideon making flour in a winepress is a significant inconsistency. Knowing this made me wonder: *Why would someone be threshing wheat in a winepress, and why is this important?*

This observation led me to study commentaries written by scholars to get their opinions. I also had to learn the agriculture practices from three thousand years ago in ancient Israel. This theological process is formally known as exegesis, or in layperson's terms, digging deeper.

Later in this book, I will explain why a young Gideon was in a winepress threshing wheat. I don't want to give away too much too early.

Soon, I took apart every line, checking through history, ancient maps, and studying ancient Hebrew, digging up every detail hidden beyond the verses we see in this wonderful story in the Bible.

In this effort, I also discovered that some of the scholars' long agreed upon theories about Gideon were incorrect. For instance, many scholars assumed God chose Gideon because he had doubts and was not very brave. Many of their writings refer to Gideon as weak or outright call him a weakling. This assumption turns out to be far from who Gideon was as a person.

What has been missed is that God referred to Gideon as a "mighty man of valor" (Judg. 6:12). Answering why God referred to Gideon this way is critical to having the proper perspective and understanding the purpose of Gideon's story.

We should always start with the knowledge that what God says is true and sacred. God is never ambiguous about truth. Knowing this made me fervently question the scholars' opinions about Gideon's weakness. While he could be viewed as weak from a societal point of view, God's opinion of him is clear.

We sometimes forget God doesn't judge us by what society says but what God sees in our hearts. God saw in Gideon a humble strength and a "mighty man of valor."

So what is it about Gideon—why did God pick him to save Israel? Through a study of history, we will discover that Gideon was the youngest son of the weakest clan of the weakest tribe of Israel. Simply put, he was seen as the lowest of all men in Israel in human societal terms. But in God's eyes, he was the one with the most valor and the perfect person to rescue Israel from evil.

Another interesting theme is how easy it is to judge the Israelites as chronically weak-minded and unfaithful to God. The continuing cycle of disobedience to God, who has to rescue them, doesn't apply only to the Israelites. The Israelites represent the entirety of the human condition with all its frailties—not just from three thousand years ago but in modern times as well.

And that is the point. Gideon's story reveals much about the human condition. It is a universal story about the ebb and flow of faith, with the constant need to overcome evil with good. These conditions have been consistent through millennia and are extraordinarily related to our lives in the twenty-first century.

In writing this book, I felt obligated to live up to the message of Gideon's story. The more I studied Gideon's character, the more I wanted to grow from the lessons of his story. Creating a passion for ensuring my facts were correct, I pushed myself to make a faithful effort to do my best and, at the same time, make the story accessible for the reader.

This effort was a fulfilling exercise of expanding my own faith. I often had to stop and ask myself if I was truly living up to the principles of Gideon's story in my writing and research. This created periods of having to stop and redo what I had written. All this was done in the effort to create a book that comprehensively reveals the magnificence of the Gideon story.

Be ready to be challenged with thoughts and events that draw you to think differently about your life. This biblical story is not to be passively read but to engage us in thinking about our own lives. The human condition is always a struggle between selfish desires and the ways of God, an eternal struggle that spans all of human history.

Faith Questions to Discuss

This story of Gideon was also written to be part of a Bible study or small group discussion. The book follows the story as told in Judges 6–8. For the most part, the dialogue used by the characters is copied directly from the Bible (NIV) to help the reader follow along. I used historical research to fill in the gaps or add more context to this story.

At the end of each chapter are faith-based questions to answer as a group or individually. The questions and answers are an essential ingredient in studying this remarkable story. There are no correct or incorrect answers. Instead, your answers are a reflection of your heart and mind that will reveal your insights into the combined human and God partnership. All the questions are designed to help with our relationship with God.

Before you start, think about the two questions below. Perhaps write a brief one-paragraph answer to each in a journal. Then as you move through the book, review your thoughts and see what has changed.

Faith Questions to Reflect on and Discuss

1. How do you view the human condition of struggling between our selfish desires and God's will?

2. How have you personally seen and experienced the eternal story of God and humankind working together?

1

A Stranger Comes to Visit

It was an early summer dawn, and Gideon was vigorously using his flail to pound the wheat sheaves he had placed in the winepress. For the last seven years, during the wheat harvest, he had performed this task at the break of dawn. In his rhythmic efforts, he found great joy, each stroke strengthening his body and increasing his endurance.

Early morning was also a time he enjoyed being alone with his thoughts. As he worked, he thought about the previous day's events and what he had to accomplish in this new day. He always took time to say silent prayers and wonder how God was working in his life. Early morning was a relaxing and centering time for him.

Gideon was a muscular man who could perform these laborious tasks with ease. Each morning he would collect the wheat sheaves, sort out the waste, and drop the good sheaves into the outdoor wine press. He threshed the wheat each morning during the harvest but was always careful and wary as he worked.

The winepress had been dug decades earlier when grapes were available, and there was no risk of the grapes being spotted and stolen. Ever since the invasion of marauders from the east, however, wine-making ceased to occur. Now the winepress, dug ten feet in the ground, was used to hide the activity of making wheat into flour.

Finding a New Home

Seven years earlier, both of Gideon's older brothers had been killed in battle when the marauders from the east invaded the land, forcing Gideon to take on many more tasks to help his father on their farm. Gideon knew he had to take the initiative to help his extended family find a new place to farm and live. His father's farm was exposed and in the open—an area the marauders could easily find and destroy.

Before he traveled into the wilderness, Gideon went to his familiar morning place to pray—a small outcrop on his farm that overlooked the valley. It was here each morning at dawn that he spent quiet time thinking about his day and praying.

His prayer this particular morning was to find a new home where his family could thrive. It had to be close enough to town and his tribe to prevent complete isolation yet hidden enough to be suitable for farming without being seen.

After praying, Gideon gathered food and water and went into the wilderness. The wilderness contained dense oak and pine trees. On the forest floor below the trees grew bushes with sharp thorns. The wilderness was a tangled and dense web of green.

It was now early summer, and the winter rains had disappeared. There would be little rain for months, and the land would turn dry and dusty.

After an easy climb to the top of a hill, he found a vantage point that would help him narrow his search.

To the south, he saw a grove of trees with yellow waving stalks of wild barley surrounding the grove. The hills surrounding the grove looked suitable for farming. He wondered if, in this hidden area, he had found a place to move.

As Gideon walked to the area he spotted on the top of the hill, he thought he saw dwellings hidden in the trees. The closer he got, the more apparent it became his eyes weren't deceiving him. He headed into the grove, and before him was an abandoned farm.

It appeared someone decades earlier had spotted the same grove and set up a place for their family. For some unknown reason, it was now abandoned. Perhaps the location was too isolated, or maybe the extended family had succumbed to disease. The reason wasn't as important to Gideon—he would make it a safe haven for his family.

The buildings, while not in great shape, were repairable. He found an extensive set of hidden terraces that could be made ready for planting and harvesting. He knew it would take hard work to resurrect the terraces, which had become overgrown with weeds. However, this hard work would be better than living in fear and scrounging the wilderness for food.

As he walked the grounds of the abandoned farm, Gideon found an old winepress. Weeds and underbrush had grown inside. When he went down into the winepress, he found he could easily remove the vegetation. The walls and floor were still in perfect shape.

The winepress, sunken ten feet into the ground, would be a perfect place to thresh wheat. He would be unseen and freed from the eyes of the marauders.

Upon emerging from the winepress, Gideon put his hands on his hips and surveyed the property. After his study, he became convinced this was a good place to live. He didn't want to merely survive and live scared while hiding in caves, like others from his tribe. He wanted a place where his family could still farm and live a somewhat normal life.

This was the place. It would require months of hard work. But what others weren't willing to do to revive this old farm, Gideon was. There would be the monotony of removing the overgrowth and long days of fixing the buildings. But he knew it was possible, and he would do his best. But first, he had to convince his father this was the right move.

After his brothers' deaths, his father also began thinking about moving deeper into the wilderness to avoid any more calamities at the hands of the invaders. His father knew danger lurked every day, but he couldn't seem to make the effort to look for a new place. For Gideon's father, the loss of his two sons and the despair of leaving his home had muted his urgency to move.

Gideon went back to his father and told him what he had found. Thankfully, his father liked what he heard and was relieved and grateful that Gideon had taken the initiative to find a new home. His father now had the urge to move forward. So, the two men went to the abandoned outpost.

Upon arriving, they walked the property without talking, looking at the overgrowth, the old buildings, and the surrounding countryside. Occasionally, Gideon's father would bend down and remove some weeds without saying a word.

Next, his father ventured to the buildings and looked closely at their condition. When he had finished surveying the property, he finally spoke, praising Gideon and telling him this place was perfect.

They agreed that this would be their new home. Over the next few months, they repaired the buildings and cleared the underbrush.

Gideon put in many hours helping his father restore the farm. The labor was hard, but his family would be safer than those who had chosen to stay put or hide in caves. If they were careful about concealing their activity, the marauders from the east would leave them alone.

A New Life in a New Home

Over the next seven years, Gideon and his extended family survived and enlarged their outpost. They enjoyed enough prosperity that ten other men showed up on the farm to help out and reside. The men were drifters displaced by the invasion and had no place else to go. They, too, had now found a place of safety.

During these seven years, Gideon grew from a slender young adult into a muscular man. His demeanor stayed quiet and reserved, never really saying much—a respectful and industrious son. During this time, Gideon also learned prayer and hard work could turn a little into a lot.

These years changed the young man. While others slept, Gideon worked around the farm and put in long days. He grew to have superb endurance. For his father, Gideon was a valued helper, one he could trust without giving much direction.

Besides growing stronger and wiser, Gideon used the early morning time to grow spiritually as well. In the still of the morning, he could be alone with his thoughts. During these times, he would pray and think about God. Though most others had moved away from God, Gideon grew closer.

He watched his prayers get answered. The answers came in unusual ways. Gideon knew the answers were meant for him because they were so unique. The more these events occurred, the better Gideon got at observing God's activities in his life.

The morning was a special time for the young man. Each night he went to sleep with anticipation of what the next day would bring. The quiet of the morning was a time Gideon relished.

Meeting the Angel of the Lord

Ironically, life got worse for most in his community, but Gideon's life improved because he was adaptable to change. Sure, he had to be more careful and work harder, but he grew stronger and closer to God.

Gideon was always excited by productive change. Worthwhile change helped Gideon become a flexible problem-solver.

Now, seven years after the marauders from the east had forced Gideon's family to move, his morning work in the winepress was an example of his approach to life. The winepress he changed into a suitable place to flail wheat was now a place he hardened himself and grew close to God. The winepress was symbolic of Gideon's adaptability, strength, and relationship with the one and only God.

The winepress was now used for a different purpose—to conceal the threshing of wheat. Situated ten feet below the ground surface and dug out to form a hidden circle, the winepress provided a safe place for Gideon to thresh the grain unnoticed. In addition, a stone wall surrounding the wine press further obscured his vigorous activity.

Each morning, Gideon warily looked at his surroundings, scrutinizing the area for strangers who might have observed his activity and any irregularities in his yard or the nearby hillsides. When he was sure it was safe, he went down into the winepress.

One day after surveying the landscape and feeling sure he was unseen, Gideon went into the old winepress with his wheat. A stranger came unnoticed and sat beneath a terebinth tree located near the winepress. The stranger waited silently.

When Gideon finished threshing and gathered the wheat, he effortlessly climbed out of the winepress and over the stone wall. Startled, he spotted the stranger. He thought he had been careful to make sure no one was around, but it appeared he hadn't been careful enough.

He silently chastised himself for making this egregious error, feeling he exposed his actions, dooming this day's work and perhaps the annual harvest.

The stranger raised his head, looked up at him, and said, "The Lord is with you, O mighty man of valor" (Judg. 6:12 ESV). Gideon narrowed his focus and suspiciously looked at the stranger. This comment bewildered and confused him. He thought to himself, *Why would the stranger tell me the Lord is with me, and how is it that he calls me a man of valor?*

He had always hoped the Lord was with him. Even though most in his community had given up on God, he hadn't. Gideon had had many prayers answered by God, and he felt God's presence in all he did.

Gideon had also watched his local leaders conceal their activities and meet at night to complain about how the Lord had abandoned them. Yet Gideon, even though he had to work harder over the last seven years, never felt personally abandoned by God. Still, he somewhat understood why the leaders had felt abandoned by God.

Questioning the stranger, he said, "Please, my Lord, if the Lord is with us, why then has all this happened to us? Where are all His wonders that our ancestors told us about when they said, 'Did not the Lord bring us up out of Egypt?' But now, the Lord has abandoned us and given us into the hand of Midian" (Judg. 6:13).

Normally Gideon was dutiful, respectful to his elders, and not this forward with his thoughts. His bold statement was driven by loyalty to his people.

He also wondered why the stranger said, "The Lord is with you." Certainly, even in the direst of times, he sought God's help and had often received an unusual but helpful response. But Gideon's prayers for his community always seemed to go unanswered. He wanted to believe the stranger. He had prayed for relief from God for his community, but few answers arrived for this prayer.

Ignoring Gideon's question, the stranger further instructed the young man, saying, "Go in this strength of yours and save Israel from the hand of Midian. Do I not send you?" (Judg. 6:14).

This comment further confused Gideon. How did this stranger know who he was? Was this a ruse by a spy? And more importantly, why would he be the one to save Israel?

As he looked deeply at the stranger, Gideon didn't sense danger. Instead, he felt sincerity. He was caught off guard, and his mind struggled to catch up with the moment.

Then a strange, powerful feeling fell over Gideon, and he believed the stranger was speaking truthfully.

He still wondered, *Who was this stranger to convey such a bold and quick message? Was this the Lord or perhaps even an angel of the*

Lord? And why does he assume I'm capable of accomplishing this wild request of saving Israel? And he wondered if the Lord had finally listened to his prayers.

He said to the stranger, "Pardon me, my Lord, but how can I save Israel? My clan is the weakest in Manasseh, and I am the least in my family" (Judg. 6:15).

The stranger replied, "I will be with you, and you will strike all the Midianites, leaving none alive" (Judg. 6:16).

Then, still somewhat skeptical but becoming hopeful that he was talking to God or an angel, Gideon replied, "If now I have found favor in your eyes, give me a sign that it is really you talking to me. Please do not go away until I come back and bring my offering and set it before you" (Judg. 6:17-18).

The stranger replied, "I will wait until you return" (Judg. 6:18).

Gideon went to his family's house, and as he walked, he felt compelled to believe the stranger was either God or an angel. After all, the stranger even knew that the marauders from the east were Midianites.

Gideon felt cautious yet compelled to press forward. He was also wary because what the stranger said about him saving Israel seemed impossible.

As Gideon prepared the offering, his mind raced; was this really a divine conversation? He thought about all those nights listening to his elders by the campfires, hearing how God had abandoned them and left them to contend with the Midianites, the marauders from the east.

There was much for Gideon to digest. Finally, overwhelmed by his racing mind, he steadied himself by focusing solely on preparing the offering for the stranger.

Faith Questions to Discuss

1. How would you have felt if the angel of the Lord called you "O mighty man of valor?" Would you have felt suspicious, affirmed, or doubtful?

2. Who was the angel of the Lord? Have you had similar visits and experiences as Gideon has had?

3. What time of day do you spend with God and why?

4. Have you ever felt abandoned by God? What was your reaction?

2

The Cycle of Decline
for the Israelites

Seven years earlier, the Midianites came from the east and invaded the Israelites' land. Like locusts, they devoured all they saw. At first, the Israelites tried to plant crops, raise livestock and make wine. However, the Midianites came and took their bounty, leaving them with nothing.

Finally, the Israelites were forced to give up their farms and go to the mountains. They lived in dens and small hideaways, concealing themselves from their enemies. They became an impoverished nation, and after seven years of oppression and defeat, they cried out to the Lord.

Now we might ask, why wait seven years to cry out? When we read the number seven in the Bible, it represents God or a period associated with God at work.

In this case, it was time for the Israelites to stop being hardheaded and disobedient to the ways of God. They had to move away from their lives of selfishness and their worship of false gods.

Like Gideon, a few of them saw that the plight was due to the Israelites' disobedience. Slowly, others would come to believe the same thing that Gideon believed. Finally, after seven years, a large enough number connected their disobedience to God's abandonment.

When they realized this, the Israelites cried out to God.

This cycle of disobedience to God and His ways was nothing new. Since the time the Israelites were released from slavery in Egypt, this cycle had occurred many times.

The Israelites would disobey God, then cry out for salvation. God would save the Israelites, and they would experience periods of peace. Before this current period of devastation, the Israelites had lived in peace for forty years under the fourth judge, Deborah.

In the Israelites' early history, after their deliverance from Egypt, their leaders were not kings or queens; they were called judges—ad hoc leaders whom God used to rescue Israel from a crisis. Twelve judges would rule for three hundred years. The reign of judges started with Joshua.

The History of the Israelites Finding God's Promised Land

Centuries earlier, Joshua had led the twelve tribes of Israel over the Jordan River to settle in the "Promised Land," which God had promised to the Israelites forty years earlier after leaving their bondage in Egypt.

Many think Moses led the Israelites over the Jordan River to the Promised Land during their exodus from slavery in Egypt. But in actuality, it was Joshua.

After leading the Israelites in the wilderness for forty years, Moses gave up his leadership of the Israelites on the banks of the Jordan River. God had previously told Moses he would not cross the Jordan River. So, despite leading the Israelites for forty years in the wilderness, Moses would not cross.

During the forty-year journey from Egypt to the Promised Land, Moses had, in a few occurrences, given into the peoples' lack of faith in God. One important time was during an attempt to cross the Jordan River into the Promised Land. Some forty years earlier, the Israelites had become fearful of crossing and protested, leading Moses to ignore God's request for the Israelites to cross the Jordan River into this Promised Land. Essentially, Moses gave into human fears instead of following God's direction.

After this event, God forced the Israelites to roam forty years in the wilderness until those who had refused to cross over into the Promised Land passed away—leaving the second generation and those under the age of twenty at the time of the first attempt to be the ones who would inherit the Promised Land.

It was during the wandering in the wilderness that God had told Moses he would not cross.

At one point during this time of wandering, the Israelites ran out of water and complained bitterly to Moses. The Israelites had lost their faith in God once again.

Moses went to God, who told Moses to strike a large rock in the area with his staff, and it would produce water. Moses complied; the rock produced an abundance of water.

It was after this event that God informed Moses he would not cross. While Moses had, for the most part, led the Israelites faithfully, these moments of doubt had cost Moses the privilege of crossing the Jordan River into the Promised Land.

Even Moses, one of history's great faith leaders, succumbed to doubt. It seems doubt is a regular part of the human condition, even with the most faithful.

After his earthly death, Moses would not disappear from history; he'd later appeared at Jesus's transfiguration. Both Elijah, the great prophet, and Moses would talk with Jesus on Mount Tabor before Jesus started His three-year mission on earth. Despite Moses's momentary lapses in faith, he was not forgotten by God.

As a young man under the age of twenty, Joshua was one of only two Israelites who'd advised Moses at the first attempt at crossing the Jordan River that it would be safe. So now Joshua, one of the few alive at the first attempt to cross, was designated by God to lead the Israelites.

Just before the second attempted crossing, Moses passed the leadership onto Joshua and went to the top of Mount Nebo, a place overlooking the Promised Land. There he died at the age of one hundred and twenty.

Joshua then led the Israelites over the Jordan River into the Promised Land, where he would be in charge for many years. At an advanced age, Joshua convened a meeting with the elders and the chiefs of the twelve tribes of Israel in Shechem.

Shechem was the quasi-capital of the Israelites. It was also part of the land given to the Israelite tribe of Ephraim. At this meeting, Joshua advised the group to stick to the ways of God and life would be good. Soon after the meeting, Joshua died.

After Joshua's death, the Israelites didn't want earthly kings and queens; the only king the Israelites wanted was God, so they called their rulers judges. Over the next three hundred years, twelve judges would rule over the Promised Land of the Israelites.

However, this period was marked by a continuous cycle of obedience to God and His ways, followed by periods of disobedience to God, causing the loss of His protection. Calamities would then occur for the Israelites, followed by a crying out to God and receiving salvation by God. Thus, an eternal cycle occurred of being oriented with God, then disoriented, and back to being reoriented.

Deborah Becomes the Fourth Judge

The judge before Gideon's time was Deborah. She became the fourth judge after God visited her and told her to rescue the Israelites from the king of Canaan, Jabin.

Jabin had invaded the land of the Israelites twenty years earlier. He was ruthless and oppressed the Israelites.

The area surrounding the land of the Israelites was inhabited by some tribes who worshipped multiple false gods and engaged in cultic practices. Prior to Deborah's reign as judge, despite the warnings of Joshua and Moses against it, the Israelites mingled with these tribes. Unfortunately, they adopted many of their practices, and God abandoned the Israelites. Without God's protection, King Jabin of Canaan invaded and conquered the land of the Israelites.

Deborah herself was an unusual selection as a judge. During the time before her rise, the priestly class of the Israelites, called the Levites, had grown corrupt. The Israelites had seen this and avoided the priests when seeking wisdom.

At the same time, Deborah had become well known to the people as a wise and honest person. When Deborah spoke, people listened. She thought less of what people would say about her and more about being faithful to God. Even when it was unfashionable, she spoke honestly and sincerely.

Deborah was a kind and compassionate person, even when she delivered harsh news, often labored over what to say instead of being blunt. Her primary goal was always to help.

It was to her that the Israelites directed their questions and requests for help. God saw the corruption of the priests and also saw Deborah's wisdom. In turn, God gave Deborah the power of prophecy. In other words, she became God's go-to when sending a message to the Israelites.

After the twenty years of oppression by King Jabin, God heard the peoples' plea and sent a message to Deborah to save Israel. This was a mighty challenge considering Jabin's great army, including nine hundred chariots.

Deborah sent for Barak, the Israelite's military commander. When he arrived at her court, he found Deborah sitting in her usual place in the open air under a palm tree. It was a place Deborah often met those visiting her. Later, that palm tree would be called the Palm of Deborah.

She calmly told Barak that God had given her a message. The message from God was for him to amass ten thousand warriors and take them to Mount Tabor to fight King Jabin. She then told Barak that God would lead Jabin's army—led by the Canaanites' great commander Sisera—to be destroyed by Barak's army.

Despite Deborah's reputation and God's involvement, Barak was afraid. Barak was more enamored with being the leader of the military than actually fighting and would avoid anything that might threaten his safety.

Nevertheless, he craftily told Deborah he would comply, but only if she joined him. When Deborah heard this very unusual request, her eyes widened, and her head went back slightly. Barak's answer was not even close to the response she expected.

Deborah was surprised by this demand and Barak's lack of faith. After a prolonged period of thinking through her next steps, she agreed to comply with Barak's request.

But first, she delivered an ominous message. She told Barak, "But because of the course you are taking, the honor will not be yours, for the Lord will deliver Sisera into the hands of a woman" (Judg. 4:9). It seems Barak's lack of faith and fear would cost him a place in history.

Barak did assemble the army, and as God had promised, Sisera's forces were led to Barak's army. With God's help, they routed the Canaanites, chasing down the nine hundred chariots and all those on foot. When Sisera the Canaanite leader saw all was doomed, he fled to a nearby oasis.

As soon as Sisera arrived at the oasis, he spotted his friend Heber's wife, Jael. He commanded her to conceal him and provide water. Jael gave him water and prepared a place for him to rest in a tent. Sisera then told her to stand by the tent opening and deny that he was there to anyone who came looking. Certain he was safe, Sisera fell into a deep sleep.

Jael was quietly sympathetic toward the Israelites. She had witnessed King Jabin's ruthless oppression of the Israelites for the last twenty years and was appalled.

When Jael was sure Sisera was asleep, she pounded a tent peg into his head, killing him.

Soon after, Barak arrived at the tent and saw that Jael had killed Sisera. Exactly as Deborah had told Barak, because of his doubt and lack of faith, the death of the great commander was not his to claim—it would be that of a woman.

Forty Years of Peace

After this victory, King Jabin was subdued, and the Israelites were free again. God compelled the Israelites to make Deborah their fourth judge, starting forty years of peace for the Israelites.

For the first few years, the priests changed and became loyal to God and His words. The priests were then heard respectfully, and the leaders were honorable and committed to serving the people.

Throughout the land, goodwill toward one another was the go-to social behavior. Farms were prosperous, and people were honest and trustworthy in their business transactions. Widows were protected, and farmers donated part of their fields to feed those short on food. A general practice was leaving a portion of their crops on the edges of the fields for those in need. Neighbors helped and protected each other.

Relieved that God and Deborah had saved them, the Israelites showed a determined effort to be a faithful community. A recommitted effort to follow the laws and ways of God prevailed throughout the land.

Life in Antiquity

During Deborah's reign in these ancient times, peril and danger were always lurking. The key tenets of loving God and your neighbor were an essential part of keeping society stable—a message that would be one of Jesus's key tenets many centuries later.

In modern times, our cities have police, EMTs, and fire responders, but during Gideon's time, these were non-existent. Neighbors took care of neighbors.

Large cities like Shechem had jails and a central government, but in smaller towns, the elders coordinated these civic responsibilities. Citizens threw bandits out of town, and neighbors put out fires.

Before the Israelites' time, Shechem had been a Canaanite enclave. Now, Shechem was the de facto capital of Israel, not Jerusalem. In the future, the Israelites would split because of a civil war over control of the throne and the places of worship. This war created two independent nations, Judah and Israel. Israel was also known as Samaria. Shechem would become the capital of Israel, and Jerusalem would rise in stature and become the holy city in Judah.

Shechem was located in an area settled by the Ephraim tribe on a bustling trade route bordered by the Jordan River. During the early part of Deborah's reign, the leaders in Shechem served the Israelites well. Although Deborah was the nation's leader, the Israelites were governed in a decentralized fashion. Tribal chiefs managed regional or tribal affairs, and towns or villages were generally no larger than four hundred people.

Extended families would cluster together, building houses with a central courtyard. A typical house was constructed with mudbricks on top of stones; if a second-floor existed, it was made of wood. The house generally had three or four rooms, with the sleeping quarters on the roof of the house, covered by a cloth canopy or timber. One of the rooms on the first floor opened to the courtyard and contained the family's livestock.

The land of the Israelites was hilly and filled with scrub brush pine, oaks, and terebinth trees. The villagers would burn off the dense growth to create a family farm. The more elaborate farms used sophisticated irrigation systems to save and control water.

Because of the hilly nature of the terrain, the Israelites created tiered terraced plots supported by stone. The terraces were used to grow crops. Each tier would be planted with vegetables or, if large enough, with grain. Some terraces would perhaps have a few trees or even a whole grove.

When someone looked up from the valley and into the hills, they would see extensive reddish-brown landscaping layered with green and yellow. The terraces rose like steps to the top of rolling hills, organized and recurrent in their structure.

Farmers had three principal tools to sow, weed, and harvest. The most common instrument was a hoe, used to break up the soil for planting or weeding. Next, a mattock was used for the more demanding activity of starting a plot. While heavier, it was more efficient in creating the terraces. The mattock could dig deeper and remove larger rocks. It was a more efficient tool for these laborious tasks.

Farms with larger terraced plots would use a simple plow pulled by a donkey, horse, or oxen. The plow, called an ard, was made of wood with either bronze or iron for the blade. The work was hard on these farms, and having many children became an asset in producing a successful crop.

Harvesting grain occurred in the spring or early summer and involved the whole community. Grain was cut and gathered on threshing floors, usually of beaten earth. Livestock would pull a heavy wooden sled, studded underneath with jagged flints, in circles over the grain. This process served to cut up the straw and crush the husks around the grains. The wheat or barley was then placed in a broad, flat winnowing basket and tossed in the air. The breeze would carry away the lighter chaff, leaving the heavy grain. Somebody later collected the discarded lighter chaff for making mud bricks or pottery.

More prosperous families had grape, fig, or olive trees growing in the courtyard or on terraces. Where grapes grew, the family compound had a sunken winepress to make wine.

Livestock wasn't in abundance, and wheat was the general crop. Most families relied on grain or fruit for nourishment. Industrious families would also grow lentils, garbanzo beans, barley, and millet.

While perfect for farming, the terraced plots worked against the Israelites when the Midianites invaded. The invaders could easily see which farms were ready to harvest and then pinpoint their raids. Now devoid of crops, these three centuries-old farms laid barren, stripped of their needed produce by the Midianites.

Even before the Midianite invasion, life was hard three millennia ago. Life was especially hard for women and children. Half of the children died before the age of ten, with a quarter dying in their first year.

Likewise, childbirth was dangerous. Even with a midwife, giving birth could be life-threatening for both mother and child.

In addition, the lack of modern-day sanitation and surgical intervention contributed to a much higher death rate than in modern times. The average life expectancy was around thirty years.

Language three thousand years ago was very complex, leading to low literacy. For example, there were no vowels, and words were written without spaces. Spaces between words would not occur until the tenth century AD. Instead, reading and writing were reserved for those who were trained in dealing with the extraordinary complexities of ancient languages.

Most writing was generally done on plant-based material in the form of scrolls. Many of these scrolls would last no longer than a few decades before having to be copied down again. Some scribes spent their entire lives rewriting the same document.

Information and traditions were communicated orally. The many lessons of life were relayed through stories or fables when smaller family groups would gather or when a speaker visited their town.

The Descent into Turning from God

For most of the forty years that Deborah reigned as a judge, prosperity and calm ruled the land. But as decades passed, cracks in morality began to appear. Leaders and chiefs became less civic-minded and served their own agendas by skillfully disguising their true intent with flowery language.

The memory of being saved by God became dimmer. Justification and rationalization became ways to work around morals and the ways of God.

Farmers wanting more profits stopped following God's command to leave a portion of their crops for the poor. One had to be wary when shopping in the bazaars of the cities. Merchants became deceptive when selling trade goods.

Goodwill amongst neighbors and clans began to dissipate. Petty complaints mushroomed into overly stated feelings of insult, further dividing the clans and tribes.

Truth became less important than narratives built on preconceived opinions and feelings. Facts that didn't support a person's belief structure were discarded.

As the leaders grew more distant from God, the people went one of two ways. They tried to garner favor with the leaders or silently stewed in frustration. People throughout the land began to align themselves with groups that thought as they did. Under the surface, the Israelites were simmering with divided loyalties and points of view.

Critical thinking was replaced with group thinking. Dominant personalities created what was fashionable to think and do. Many times, these were the opposite of the ways of God. Revenge and acrimony replaced goodwill and thoughtfulness.

Mistakes were judged too harshly, and forgiveness became an afterthought. Instead of seeing each other as good people with flaws, the flaws became amplified. Most forgot that God sees the best in each person.

The priests, too, were affected by this changing tide. They began to assume a popular political stance and had less to say about moral codes. As a result, they failed to remain relevant in society. And most importantly, the Ten Commandments became twisted legalistically to support the dominant group's viewpoints.

After a few decades, decay had set in. Harvests were smaller. The Israelites became a divided and argumentative group. Instead of turning back to God and His ways, many Israelites turned to human-created gods to improve their lives and circumstances.

In Gideon's town and many others, people constructed two altars, one for Baal and Asherah. These human-created gods were thought to provide more wealth, and at first, were considered equal with God. As time passed, people chose Baal and Asherah over God. As a result, talking about and worshipping God became irrelevant and socially unacceptable.

Baal was a god invented by a few of the barbaric nomadic tribes that roamed the area surrounding Canaan. Often Baal was represented in a bull's form and was thought to create and increase prosperity. Later civilizations had Baal morphing into Zeus for the Greeks and Jupiter for the Romans.

Asherah was a goddess, and like Baal, was a creation of the nomadic tribes. To these idols, the Israelites had now turned in times of need. They were guilty of disobeying the first commandment: "Thou shalt have no other Gods before me."

More than a millennium later, Jesus would say, "No one could serve two masters. Either you will hate the one and love the other, or you will be devoted to the one and despise the other. You cannot love both God and money" (Matt. 6:24). Over the span of history, no statement has been truer.

To benefit themselves materially, the Israelites turned to these false gods, effectively moving away from God's moral and ethical values to gain just a little more. Ironically, the material things the false gods offered never lasted, leaving the worshipper far worse off and more desperate than before.

This movement away from God didn't happen overnight; it took two generations of a slow, insidious reduction of morality. People became less generous in helping the poor. The leaders stopped worrying if they were serving the Lord and the citizens. They became more concerned with their personal wealth and power. Even in society as a whole, talking about God became unfashionable, and some took great offense to any mention of God.

Most of society started seeking personal gain, pushing God down the list of priorities. As a result, the voices of the faithful were no longer being heard, leaving God to abandon the Israelites once again.

Ironically, God had a long history of saving the Israelites, and they turned from God each time. Thus, new generations would have to relearn history. After the demise of King Jabin, followed by forty years of peace, the Israelites had once again turned away from God. What followed was Deborah's death and seven years of oppression, destruction, and scarcity caused by the Midianites. The Israelites were once again in need of salvation.

Before the Midianites' invasion, Gideon often wondered why the elders in his community would worship Baal and Asherah instead of God. When the community would gather at night, he would hear their talk and curiously think about this irony. To himself, Gideon would say, *Why is it that these wise men would go to other gods despite the long history of God's salvation?* However, he never felt he could bring these questions up.

Gideon knew from experience that sin is an easy trap to fall into—a trap that lures you deeper with the promise of satisfaction. Only when it is too late does sin reveal the mistake. Worshipping false gods was similar, an alluring attraction that binds until calamity hits.

As a young man, Gideon was in no position to speak comfortably. He was the youngest of his father's children, and his father was low on the social ladder. His clan, the Abiezrites, were the weakest of his tribe, the Manasseh. And the Manasseh was the lowest of the twelve tribes of Israel. As a result, Gideon was at the very bottom of society and had no voice.

Faith Questions to Discuss

1. Why did it take the Israelites seven years to call out to God after the Midianites invaded? Was it stubbornness, lack of faith, or an unwillingness to give up false gods?

2. How and why did things change during Deborah's reign, and are there similarities to contemporary society?

3. Why did the leaders of Israel turn to false idols to worship despite God's long history of salvation?

4. What are some of society's false gods today? What false gods exist in your life?

3

The Midianites Invade
the Promised Land

Seven years earlier, without God's protection, the Promised Land was invaded by the Midianites. They made life miserable for the Israelites. Ironically, the name Midian in Hebrew means "strife"—not a very subtle message from God.

After the invasion, early attempts by the Israelites to live a normal life failed. Each time they planted a crop, the Midianites stole the harvest. As a result, for seven years, the Israelites were near starvation.

Gideon's family had also endured a great tragedy during the Midianites' initial invasion. Gideon's brothers had been captured and then killed near Mount Tabor. After their capture, Zebah and Zalmunna, the Midianites' two kings, refused to spare Gideon's two brothers. This act would profoundly affect the two kings in the future.

After his brothers' death, Gideon and his father fled higher into the mountains with their family. They found an abandoned outpost and moved in. Gideon and his father, unlike their neighbors, refused to give in to the terror. Instead, they created a new life—one mostly free from terror. When others resigned themselves to hiding and despair, Gideon's family led a somewhat normal life because of Gideon's prayers and hard work.

They were far luckier than the other townspeople who waited, hoping things would get better—many of these same people were later forced to find refuge in dens in the mountains.

If Gideon and his father, Joash, were careful, their family could raise crops and livestock without being spotted by the Midianites.

But the life of their neighbors and other Israelites progressively got worse. Despite all their efforts to survive, the Israelites were close to becoming a finished nation.

God Delivers a Tough Message

After seven years of the Midianites' oppression, the Israelites had no place to turn. The few voices of those who remained loyal to God began to be heard—no longer pushed to the side by those who had ignored them in the previous decades. So the Israelites finally and desperately cried out to the Lord for help.

In response, God sent a message to the Israelites through a prophet who said, "This is what the Lord, the God of Israel, says: I brought you up out of Egypt, out of the land of slavery. I rescued you from the hand of the Egyptians. And I delivered you from the hand of all your oppressors; I drove them out before you and gave you their land. I said to you, 'I am the Lord your God; do not worship the gods of the Amorites, in whose land you live.' But you have not listened to me" (Judg. 6:8–10).

The message had been delivered, and the Israelites were still a desperate people. God uses tough situations to get people's attention.

The Amorites mentioned by the prophet of God were predecessors of the nomadic tribes that roamed the Middle East. They wandered the area from Mesopotamia to Egypt a millennium earlier. Over time, they became splintered and morphed into many nomadic tribes. Their legacy included creating false gods like the ones God warned the Israelites to avoid.

The Midianites' History Intertwined with the Israelites

The Midianites that invaded Gideon's homeland had a long history with the Israelites. But first, we should know they were an offshoot of one of Abraham's sons.

God had blessed Abraham and his wife Sarah with a son named Isaac. After Issacs's birth, Abraham took a second wife, Keturah, who had six children. The fourth was named Midian. While Abraham was kind to his other children, he did not treat them as equal to Isaac.

As a side note, Isaac was not Abraham's first son; that title belongs to Ishmael—a son Abraham had with Hagar, his wife's servant. After losing faith in God's promise that he and Sarah would have a son, he pursued Hagar, his wife's servant. Sarah gave Abraham permission to have a son with Hagar, and Ishmael was born.

Even though Abraham showed a lack of faith in God's promise, he and Sarah did eventually have a son, Isaac, despite Abraham being almost ninety years old.

Abraham had eight children: Isaac with Sarah, Ismael with Haggar, and Midian and five other children with Keturah. When Abraham died, only Isaac and Ishmael attended his funeral. And only Isaac received an inheritance from Abraham. It seems Abraham, the father of the Judeo-Christian faith, played favorites.

The other sons of Abraham were sent away to the east, including Midian. For future generations, this would continue to affect history. Midian's offspring, the Midianites, would be closely involved with the Israelites for many years, usually in a detrimental way. They became lawless people who ignored God and roamed the desert. Never having a land of their own, they raided and pillaged to obtain food and livestock.

The Midianites knew camels were crucial for roaming and pillaging. When many other nomadic tribes only had donkeys, the Midianites had camels. These animals allowed them to travel days without the need to stop for water. The Midianites had so many camels, some would say they were too numerous to count. These camels gave the Midianites an advantage in travel speed, allowing them to roam and pillage efficiently.

Centuries before Gideon's time, the Midianites discovered Isaac's grandson, Joseph, in a pit. His older brothers put him there in an act of jealousy. The Midianites took Joseph to Egypt and sold him to the captain of Pharaoh's guard.

Unwittingly, by selling Joseph to the Egyptians, the Midianites set up the events that created the formation of the twelve tribes of Israel.

The Israelites Time in Egypt

After a few years as a slave and being imprisoned, Joseph became a key advisor to Pharaoh. Pharoah had heard about Joseph's wisdom and invited him to serve. Joseph quickly became a trusted advisor and had a powerful influence in Egypt.

Later, he became a benefactor to his eleven brothers during a great famine. In the land where his brothers lived, a great famine occurred. Their father and Isaac's son, Jacob, sent the eleven to Egypt to buy food. During this visit, they became reunited with Joseph.

Joseph overcame his anger at being put in a pit and invited his eleven brothers to settle in Egypt during the famine. The desperate eleven brothers accepted the invitation and settled in Egypt.

These eleven sons, plus Joseph, were the twelve sons of Jacob and are the namesakes of the twelve tribes of Israel. Gideon's tribe, the Manasseh, was actually a half-tribe. Along with the Ephraim tribe, they combined to make up the twelfth tribe or the tribe representing Joseph.

This seems a little complicated but can be explained as follows. Jacob had asked Joseph on his death bed if his two sons,

Ephraim and Manasseh, could be given the inheritance of the twelfth tribe. Joseph agreed out of respect for his father. So, Joseph's sons were each given half a share of Joseph's birthright.

So why are they called the twelve tribes of Israel when they represent Jacob's sons?

Earlier, Jacob had wrestled with God in the desert and injured his hip. After this fight, God changed Jacob's name to Israel. The word Israel means "contends or struggles with God" in Hebrew. In the long history of the Israelites' relationship with God, the name certainly applies, as it does for all humankind.

From a historical context, we must also remember the Israelites at least contended with God when many of the other people of this time ignored or had no relationship with God. Therefore, our judgment of the Israelites should be tempered with this knowledge.

And we should bear in mind that many times, it was the leaders of the Israelites, tempted by power and money, who led the people astray. Their actions helped cause the historical ebb and flow of their relationship with God.

This is the origin of the nation of Israel and the formation of the Israelites, the twelve sons of Jacob (Israel), and their many descendants. Manasseh, Gideon's tribe and birth lineage, was considered the weakest.

What the Midianites had done out of profit unwittingly created the course of events that eventually gave rise to the twelve tribes of Israel, the formation of Judeo–Christianity, and a linkage from Abraham to Jesus.

Moses Rescues the Israelites

Initially, when the Israelites lived in Egypt after Joseph's invitation, they prospered and multiplied. However, as they prospered, Egypt's people grew jealous, and later Pharaoh enslaved the Israelites. Once the Israelites became enslaved, they provided a significant source of wealth to the Egyptians, and the Israelites still continued to grow in size.

At the time of Moses's birth, Pharaoh saw that the Israelites, though enslaved, continued their population growth. This concerned Pharaoh, who then wanted to limit the Israelites' further expansion; he was fearful that they would rise up and rebel.

In response to this fear, Pharaoh ordered all newborn Israelite boys to be murdered. To avoid having her son murdered, Moses's mother put him in a basket and set him amongst the reeds in the Nile River, hoping a kind person would rescue her son. Here is an interesting twist in this story: Pharaoh's daughter saved Moses and made him part of her family.

Moses grew up in a house of wealth and among royalty. However, as a young adult, he saw an Egyptian slave-master harassing an Israelite. In a fit of anger, Moses killed the Egyptian. To avoid being captured and imprisoned because of this act of rage, he fled across the Red Sea to an area occupied by the Midianites.

Here Moses met Jethro, one of the few honest men of the Midianites. Unlike other Midianites, Jethro lived on a farm in a section of the Sinai Peninsula. Jethro was also a high priest and provided counsel to many in his community. Moses married his daughter and stayed on Jethro's farm until God called him to rescue the Israelites.

Later, Moses would meet God in the form of a burning bush while he was tending Jethro's sheep. In this conversation, God asked Moses to lead the enslaved Israelites to "a land of milk and honey." A Promised Land for the Israelites.

Reluctantly, Moses agreed and convinced Pharaoh to release the Israelites. It did, however, take ten God-created plagues to convince Pharaoh to free the Israelites. Moses then led the twelve tribes of Israel to the edge of the Jordan River from Egypt to their Promised Land of milk and honey.

As we now know, Moses never crossed over the Jordan River into the Promised Land occupied by the Israelites. Instead,

Moses died on top of Mount Nebo, overseeing the land given to the Israelites by God. Joshua, Moses's protégé, took the final steps in settling the Israelites in the land given to them by God.

Throughout the long history of the Israelites, the Midianites were often near—an ever-present danger from a lawless people, far from God, that roamed the Middle East. Now the Midianites, whose own history was intertwined with the Israelites' history, had invaded the land of Canaan, the Israelites' Promised Land from God.

Faith Questions to Discuss

1. What is the Promised Land for the Israelites? What is your Promised Land?

2. Who are the Midianites? What or whom do they represent metaphorically?

3. The name Israel means "contend or struggle with God." When and how do you contend or struggle with God?

4

Gideon Destroys the Altar of Baal

Gideon was always reserved in his comments and careful when he smiled. He sat quietly when the men of his community spoke. Gideon listened carefully, often not agreeing with what he heard and believing others wouldn't listen to him if he did talk.

If you studied Gideon closely, you would find an uncommon depth and intellect. After years of being the least, he spoke little. When he did, he was careful with his words. Gideon always looked carefully at the listener to gauge their reaction when he did speak. He was a quiet man on the surface, which hid his deep faith and intellect.

Even though Gideon was ignored because of his low social status, he was always respectful and thoughtful to his neighbors, family, and friends. Gideon didn't act toward others as he was treated. Instead, he was respectful to others, as God wanted him to be. While most let others rule their lives and thoughts, Gideon chose God to rule his life.

This physical, moral, and intellectual strength is what the angel of the Lord saw in Gideon—which explains why Gideon was called a "mighty man of valor" by the angel of the Lord.

Even when others didn't see Gideon this way, the angel of the Lord did.

The angel of the Lord knew Gideon thought about God and His ways when others would think about how to survive in human terms. Likewise, Gideon turned to God's words to find the truth when others would debate. While the men in his community had long ago forgotten to rely on God, Gideon talked silently with God to find his answers.

He knew the men and leaders of his community were far off the path of living with God but kept these thoughts to himself, feeling he had to be silent.

Gideon also spent much time in prayer, asking God why things happened. Other times he would pray for help in his tasks around the farm and for his community.

Just as importantly, Gideon keenly observed God's responses to his prayers. They were never direct or apparent answers but unusual and strange responses. Yet, these varied and unique answers helped Gideon know they were a response from God to his prayers. He had also found that the more patient he was in his observations, the clearer the answers became.

Gideon gained confidence when he knew God was involved. When others tried to use their human abilities, Gideon would turn to God to help solve complex dilemmas.

Gideon learned how to distinguish between coincidence and providence. He felt emboldened when he knew it was God. Deep joy would fill him when he knew God was listening. In these times, he would look up toward the sky, filled with praise, and say, "I know that was you, God." In these times, his prayers turned from seeking help to prayers of thanksgiving. One prayer not yet answered was how God would save his people.

Gideon Prepares a Feast for the Angel of the Lord

Gideon continued preparing the stranger's offering, consisting of a young goat, broth, and bread. The bread alone weighed thirty-six pounds; this was a grand feast. Then, leaving his house, he went up to the stranger and showed him the offering.

The stranger, still sitting under the terebinth tree, eyed what Gideon had brought him. Then, after a few quiet moments, he lifted his head and said to Gideon, "Take the meat and the unleavened bread, place them on this rock, and pour out the broth" (Judg. 6:20).

Gideon, at first, was confused. He had brought out a grand meal for the stranger, and now he wanted him to place it aside on a rock. Despite his confusion, Gideon still complied with this strange request.

Carefully, he poured out the broth and set the bread and meat on the rock. The stranger effortlessly rose from under the tree and moved toward the meal. With the tip of his staff, the stranger touched the meal. Suddenly, bright fire burst forth, emitting a heavenly light. Gideon saw the meal had been consumed when the dazzling light's effect died down.

Gideon's eyes widened, and he was stunned by the event. Immediately, his doubt about the stranger disappeared. Gideon became afraid and said, "Alas, Sovereign Lord! I have seen the angel of the Lord face to face!" (Judg. 6:22). He was nervous because he had heard the story of when Moses spoke to the Lord many years earlier: God had told Moses, "You cannot see my face because no one can see me and live" (Exod. 33:20).

Sensing this fear, the angel turned his eyes to Gideon and said, "Peace! Do not be afraid. You are not going to die" (Judg. 6:23). Relieved and filled with joy, Gideon built an altar to the Lord. Today, this altar stands in Ophrah, Gideon's hometown, called The Lord Is Peace. The altar, made of gray stone blocks, stands just under five feet high and is formed into a square.

The angel of the Lord was pleased with Gideon's altar and disappeared. Gideon returned to his chores and spent the rest of the day thinking about this odd but wonderful visit from the angel of the Lord.

Gideon Tears Down the Altar of Baal

After dark, the angel of the Lord revisited Gideon, delivering another message, which was very specific:

"Take the second bull from your father's herd, the one seven years old. Tear down your father's altar to Baal and cut down the Asherah pole beside it. Then build a proper kind of altar to the Lord your God on the top of this height. Using the wood of the Asherah pole that you cut down, offer the second bull as a burnt offering" (Judg. 6:25–26).

In his youth, Gideon had wondered why his father and the townspeople had built these two altars. He had always believed that his God was not Baal or Asherah. When Gideon had listened to the older men, he always wanted to tell them they were wrong, but it wasn't his place. In these times, because of his youth and social status, he could only listen and wonder. Now, after all these years, he firmly knew his youthful intuitions had been correct.

Gideon gathered all ten of his father's laborers and told them his plan. These ten men had arrived to help his family over the last seven years and were destitute from losing their farms to the Midianites or wanderers. Luckily, Gideon and his father found one of the better plots in the wilderness and enjoyed a modest amount of prosperity, enough to support having these ten men work on the farm.

All of the ten men liked Gideon. They found him even-handed and non-judgmental. In the past, other overseers they had worked for looked only at their mistakes, never really forgetting their past and constantly reminding them of their failures.

Gideon was a different type of overseer; he saw the potential in these men. Gideon knew they would make mistakes, but they were more inclined to do good work. So instead of viewing them as failures, Gideon saw them as valued. In turn, they became immensely loyal to Gideon.

These men were loyal to Gideon because of the way he talked and worked with them. But, like Gideon, they also wondered why the elders worshipped Baal and Asherah.

Gideon felt he had to do what the angel asked that very night and not wait until the next day. He knew his father would stop him if he did what the angel of the Lord asked of him in the light of the day. He was also concerned about the reaction in town. Gideon chose to perform his task in darkness.

Gideon selected the second bull from his father's herd. The most prominent or first bull was being fattened to become a sacrifice to Baal. The angel wanted Gideon to have nothing to do with this bull, even if it was stronger. Gideon was obedient to the angel's request.

The group—ten men, the bull, and Gideon—went into the town. It was a dark night with no moon, and as they went, they spoke little to each other. They hoped to go into town unnoticed.

As they entered the town, Gideon nervously wondered if he was doing the right thing, slinking off in the middle of the night. There was much at risk for him. What he was doing seemed so unreal. He finally calmed when a feeling of peace settled over him.

When Gideon arrived at the two altars, he harnessed one end of the rope to the bull and tied the other end around the altar of Baal. Gideon put a blanket over the altar to deaden the noise when it collapsed. Then he told the ten men to stand behind the altar and push when he led the bull to pull. It didn't take much to topple the altar. The altar was weak like the promises of Baal. Falling to the ground, it broke into many pieces.

Next, the men and Gideon cut down the Asherah pole. Then they cut the pole into pieces for fuel to burn on the new altar. They gathered up the stones which had fallen from the Baal altar, then layered the stones in a way that would make the new altar to God stronger and far more substantial than the previous altar.

Gideon brought the second bull to the altar. The group concealed the area with blankets, hoping to prevent the fire from emitting any light that could be seen. Gideon lit a fire under the wood from the Asherah pole and sacrificed the bull. When the fire had consumed the bull, Gideon led the men in prayer to honor God. They left quietly and returned to the farm.

In the morning, the people emerged from their sleep and went outside. They spotted the change in the place where Gideon had done his work. They noticed the altar to Baal had been destroyed and the Asherah pole had been cut down. In their place was the new altar and the residue of the burnt offering.

As each person arrived at the scene, they became angry and demanded to know who had torn down the altar to Baal?

Gideon had tried to be quiet and unseen the night before. However, a villager had heard the altar fall and watched Gideon light the fire that consumed the bull. This one villager would erase the efforts of Gideon to hide his nocturnal activities.

At first, the villager was afraid to tell the others what he had seen. Then, knowing he could elevate himself in his neighbors' eyes, he told them everything he had seen, exposing Gideon to great wrath.

The townspeople went to see Joash. They wanted vengeance. The crowd grew larger and angrier, demanding Gideon be brought out of the house.

Joash told the crowd to wait; he would come back and address them. Joash went to Gideon and asked him what had happened. While nervous, Gideon felt compelled to tell his father everything with no tales or excuses that would save him from the angry mob.

He told his father about the angel, the prepared feast consumed by the heavenly light, and the request to destroy the altar. Gideon revealed every detail of the previous night and day.

Joash knew his son well. He knew that Gideon had silently disagreed with him and the other men about worshipping Baal. He knew his son would wander off and meditate on the ways and words of God. He also knew Gideon, while quiet, would not mislead him. Joash believed his son and needed to find a way to quiet the mob.

Joash stepped out of the house and spoke to the crowd. He relayed what Gideon had told him and asserted he believed his son. The townspeople knew Gideon's love for God and his silent, humble manner, creating doubt in their minds as well. Joash cautioned them to be careful with protecting Baal and seeking revenge. In stating his case, he said to the crowd, "If Baal really is a god, he can defend himself when someone breaks down his altar" (Judg. 6:31).

The townspeople saw the logic in Joash's plan: Let Baal defend himself. The townspeople then gave Gideon another name, Jerub-Baal, meaning "let Baal contend with him." Over 3,100 years later, the *Smithsonian Magazine*'s July 2021 edition reported that archaeologists have recently found this name written on a pottery fragment in Israel.

They all waited to see what Baal would do throughout that day and into the night. As the hours wore on and no retribution against Gideon occurred, the people became less sure Baal would come and defend himself.

This imaginary god never did show up. By the following morning, many had changed their view of Gideon. He went from being a dangerous inciter of an imaginary god to a hero with great faith in the only real God.

After these events, Gideon's father saw he had been wrong about not worshipping God. He was proud of Gideon and told him, "God gives big people big tasks."

Faith Questions to Discuss

1. Why did Gideon's community not listen to him? Do you have similar experiences in your life?

2. Who are Baal and Asherah? Are there similarities to these false gods in your life?

3. What times in your life have you acted in ways similar to Gideon tearing down the statues of the false gods? What were the consequences?

4. In the past, has God given you very specific directions? How did you react?

5

Gideon Tests God
Two More Times

Around the same time Gideon destroyed the altars in Ophrah, his hometown, the two Midianite kings met to discuss the state of their efforts to eliminate the Israelites. Their attempts to eradicate them always fell short. They saw how the Israelites fled to the wilderness and, while not thriving, were at least surviving. It was time to bring in help and launch a major attack to finally eliminate them.

To accomplish this task, the two kings of the Midianites, Zebah and Zalmunna, wanted an enormous army. They invited other tribes of the east to assist in their final plan. While there was risk in bringing in other barbarian tribes, the kings believed the benefits would greatly outweigh the risks.

Adding new tribes would create unfamiliarity within the army and potentially cause confusion. Especially during battle, the new warriors might not know who was an ally or foe. However, the kings theorized this weakness would be overcome by the size of their new army of one hundred and thirty-five thousand warriors—an army they thought more than sufficient to completely wipe out the Israelites.

The Amalekites Join the Midianites to Eliminate the Israelites

One tribe that was asked to join was the Amalekites, who had a long history of war against the Israelites. This tribe was an offshoot of Esau, the older brother of Jacob (later named Israel) and the first son of Isaac. So again, we find a relative intertwined in the story.

Esau was primarily driven by primeval means. When he was born, he was covered with an unusual amount of hair and grossly red. Esau in Hebrew means hairy. As a youth, he spent his time roaming the wilderness and working his father's fields. Esau was a primal being, always seeking to satisfy his human desires.

As the eldest son, he was entitled to inherit Isaac's wealth and become the family leader. However, it is essential to note that Esau and Jacob were twins, with Esau being born just before Jacob. So, Jacob was not the oldest son but still managed to inherit Esau's birthright. Here is how:

On a day when Esau was exhausted from working in the fields, he went into the family kitchen and saw Jacob cooking a meal of red stew. Famished and tired, Esau asked his brother to share what he was preparing. In exchange, Jacob asked for Esau's birthright. After a quick exchange, Esau relented and gave Jacob his birthright. Desperate and exhausted, he allowed his primal needs to control him.

Later Esau felt betrayed by Jacob and demanded his birthright back. Jacob refused and held Esau to his commitment. When Esau saw he could not get his birthright back, he despised his birthright. He married two women from Canaan, starting an offshoot called the Amalekites and a centuries-long rivalry with the Israelites. Esau and his ancestors never forgot the presumed betrayal by Jacob.

During the exodus from Egypt to the Promised Land, the Amalekites had constantly harassed the Israelites and threatened their existence. In one battle, Moses sent Joshua to fight the Amalekites. Moses observed how God was helping the Israelite army from a hillside during the battle. Every time Moses raised his arms and staff, God helped the Israelites gain progress in the battle. When he dropped his arms from fatigue, the Israelites would get pushed back. Fighting through the fatigue, Moses kept his arms up, and the Israelites won the battle.

Now, many years later, Esau's descendants were being given another chance to avenge Jacob's perceived deception of his older brother, Esau.

Midianites, Amalekites, and other nomadic tribes joined forces to put an end to the Israelites, becoming a mighty power of one hundred thirty-five thousand warriors that seemed too big for the Israelites to resist against.

Gideon Becomes a Nation's Hero

Gideon, who once was ignored, began to be heard. His act against Baal lifted his once weak social status to that of a leader. He could now enter conversations with the other members of his clan and tribe. His wise and unhurried voice of reason became a source of wisdom. He was no longer residing in the back when the men gathered at night to discuss the items affecting the community. Instead, Gideon was invited to the front and would receive inviting looks to give his opinion when complex subjects came up.

He even began to get questions about God. Some would tell him quietly that they, too, had not forgotten God. This was remarkable after years of people thinking that talking about God was unfashionable. This gave Gideon even greater joy than being heard by the elders. He knew the Israelites dramatic change of heart would help them once again become aligned with God.

He became more confident in what he thought. He no longer questioned himself and stopped wondering why his views seemed odd to others.

As he spoke up, people began to see he was without agenda. He unhurriedly gave his opinion with controlled oratory. The men listened earnestly; they learned what Gideon had to say wasn't self-serving but objective and carefully thought out. His family and neighbors began to see what God saw in Gideon, a "mighty man of valor." His fame and reputation grew throughout Israel. They also wondered if Gideon was the answer to their desperate plea to God for salvation.

Gideon Inspires the Israelites to Defend Their Nation

During the next few days, Gideon wondered about the angel who had visited him. While Gideon knew to be patient in waiting for the angel, it still seemed odd he hadn't had another experience. That night as he went to sleep, he prayed to know what was next.

In the still of the following morning, the Spirit of God came over Gideon and summoned him. This was not just a Spirit of prophecy; it was also a Spirit of courage and wisdom. The Spirit gave him the knowledge that his land and people were in grave danger, but the Spirit also gave him the courage to succeed, so long as he and the Israelites kept God close.

After experiencing the Spirit of God and without hesitation, Gideon went into town. He had to summon the members of his clan to tell them about his message from the Spirit and develop a plan.

In the center of town was a horn from a ram; blowing in this horn would bring the leaders of his community. The ram's horn or *shofar* was essential to the Israelite community. In a time of no phones, internet, or texting, the shofar was the community messaging system.

Traditionally, the shofar was blown over one hundred times during the holy period of Rosh Hashanah, each time with either a short burst or a prolonged one. These varying bursts let the people know what was next in celebrating Rosh Hashanah.

The shofar was also used to bring people to the center of town. The person wanting to have a meeting would blow a long, loud blast, called a *tekiah*. While the tekiah sound was also used in religious ceremonies, it could also signal that something was up and the people should meet.

Gideon, with a great breath, blew a *tekiah* from the shofar. Quickly, the leaders of his town and clan gathered. They circled around Gideon to hear what he had to say. Then, farther off, other clan members and town members gathered in groups and waited to hear what Gideon had told the leaders.

This was a very unusual event, and the townspeople knew something big was being announced. Gideon told the leaders that he had received a message from the Spirit of the Lord letting him know the Midianites had grown larger and were preparing one final attack on all of the Israelites. Gideon told them the Israelites were in grave danger.

Gideon also relayed that the Midianites, as a group, were north in the far end of the Jezreel Valley. They had set up a camp, and from there, they would infiltrate the land and destroy all they saw.

The leaders of his clan and town heard this message and began to gather up the men of the community to go with Gideon to fight the Midianites. Gideon's message had both informed and sparked action by his community.

Next, Gideon sent messengers to the north to inform the three neighboring tribes: Asher, Zebulun, and Naphtali. These tribes bordered the Jezreel valley and would be closest to the Midianites.

The leaders from the three tribes went to meet with Gideon. As Gideon had told his tribe about the grave danger, he also told the three tribal leaders.

Much had been heard about Gideon's encounters with God, making it easier for him to be heard. People had also heard about Gideon's wisdom and thoughtfulness. None of the leaders held any hesitation. They, too, went back to their communities to find men who would help Gideon and God fight the Midianites.

By now, Gideon's story about destroying the altar to Baal had made him a folk hero. The story had spread fast throughout his land. The tribes of the Israelites, after their desperate struggle for seven years, were eager and easily convinced. Many hoped Gideon, as their leader, was the answer to their cry to God for help.

Interestingly, Gideon did not meet with the Ephraim tribal leaders, the tribe with which Manasseh shared being one of the twelve tribes of Israel. Even though the warriors of Ephraim were known for being fierce and strong, Gideon purposely ignored this tribe. Because they were also known as haughty and suspicious of any leader not from their tribe, Gideon did not speak with the Ephraim leaders, knowing he would be rebuffed. This decision would later create an uncomfortable moment for Gideon.

Gideon was amazed and somewhat startled at the new loyalty shown to him by the people of his land. In almost an instant, he had gone from being nobody to a hoped-for leader. The new state of being respected was hard for Gideon to grasp completely.

After years of feeling suppressed, being heard made him feel off-balanced. Intellectually, he understood the sudden change. However, emotionally he struggled to reconcile the tribal leaders' past behavior with this newfound attention.

Gideon knew what had been unleashed—a now-desperate nation wanting to be released from oppression, a nation that felt Gideon would be their answer.

Gideon Tests God Twice

However, Gideon wanted to be sure he was on the right track and not delusional. He was concerned that he was overestimating his value to the Israelite nation. Gideon knew he had to be correct about what he had heard from the angel of the Lord. His next steps were bold and unusual.

As he usually did when he needed clarity, Gideon prayed to the Lord, saying, "If you save Israel by my hand as you have promised—look, I will place a wool fleece on the threshing floor. If there is dew only on the fleece and all the ground is dry, then I will know that you will save Israel by my hand, as you said" (Judg. 6:36–37).

This request was not a lack of faithfulness on Gideon's part. He was always an obedient servant of the Lord. He needed encouragement and to be sure he was on the right path. He also knew the answer to his prayer would show the people that God had answered once again, strengthening their faith.

Gideon carefully laid the fleece on the threshing floor in the winepress at dusk. He let others know what he asked of the Lord so they, too, could see the power of God.

When Gideon got up the next morning, he anxiously and quickly went to the threshing floor with the men from the farm. The fleece was saturated with dew, and the surrounding area was dry. When Gideon squeezed the fleece, he had a bowlful of water. Gideon sat down with relief.

Working this closely with God was a new experience for Gideon. He certainly had stayed close to God in the past, and his prayers had been answered in unusual ways. However, this event was different and much more significant. These were hands-on interactions with no subtleties in the responses from God.

While he was sure it was God, these very direct messages from God were a bit startling. These very close interactions were so different from his previous life. Now he was hearing from

God boldly. In the past, the answers to his prayers were more veiled, requiring him to think through what they meant. Now they were straightforward and very obviously from God. These answers from God brought great excitement but seemed unreal at the same time. God was working with him; this was big, and he knew it.

To further cement in his mind and to the people of Israel that he wasn't delusional and that it wasn't ego driving him to believe, Gideon humbly went back to God for one more test. He said to God, "Do not be angry with me. Let me make just one more request. Allow me one more test with the fleece, but this time make the fleece dry and let the ground be covered with dew" (Judg. 6:39–40).

Once again, Gideon told others about this second request and went to sleep filled with anticipation. He arose the next morning, and when he went outside, he saw God had spread dew all around, and the fleece was dry. This time Gideon had gone to sleep sure this request would be answered, and when he woke, he wasn't surprised by what he saw. He firmly knew now that the Lord was with him, his tribe, and all the tribes of Israel.

Gideon felt he had accomplished his goal of making sure no one would doubt God was involved. He thought to himself, *Surely now no one will question this is real.*

Gideon was thankful God was patient with him during this period of his faith development. Gideon had seen this patience from God in the past as he'd learned to pray and observe the responses. Now God's patience was clear, and Gideon was strengthened in his faith.

Upon hearing the story of the fleece, the people of Israel were further emboldened. Thoughts of despair were replaced with hope. Their former worship of Baal and Asherah was a distant memory. The Israelites knew their enemies were more powerful than them, but remembering the past stories of how God had saved them, many were ready to help.

The call to action by the messengers was spread throughout the land, and many wanted to be part of Gideon's and God's army.

Faith Questions to Discuss

1. Why did Gideon test God twice with the fleece? Was it a lack of faith, a need for reassurance, or essential for others to know God was present?

2. When you pray and see a response from God, does it seem real?

3. Who affects how you feel about yourself? Is it those around you or God?

4. How has God been patient with you?

6

Gideon Selects the Three Hundred

Gideon went to the Spring of Harod to await the arrival of warriors who would fight the Midianites with him. West of the Jordan River and east of Gideon's town, the spring was a familiar gathering spot for the people of the Manasseh tribe.

The spring sprung forth from within a cave at the bottom of Mount Gilboa. In early summer, it was a tranquil place dotted by wildflowers and surrounded by Eucalyptus trees. The water from the spring created a pool large enough for many to swim, providing relief from the heat of the day.

Because it was early summer, the effect of a rainy winter could still be seen in the area. The soft pastels of the grasses and flowers soothed those who visited. However, the summer's heat would soon dry the flowers and grasses, turning everything except for the area just around the spring-fed pool into a field of yellow-brown.

The water flowed from the spring-fed pool over a bed of rocks down into the Jezreel Valley, which spanned east into the Jordan River valley. The valley was a crossroad for those heading west into Galilee.

Many years later, it would be a site where the Philistines would defeat King Saul—a future time when another leader would lead the Israelites astray and away from God.

At the far end of the valley, a few miles in the distance, the Midianites and the other barbaric tribes from the east gathered to set up camp. All told, there would be one hundred and thirty-five thousand barbarians in this tranquil place. It would soon witness a great struggle between God and evil.

Gideon arrived at the Spring of Harod with his friends and father. Shortly after arriving, Gideon found a quiet place by the spring to sit alone and review his thoughts. He sat on the ground, resting on a fallen log, round enough to make it a comfortable place to sit. This would be one of his few quiet moments in the upcoming weeks. For now, being out of the mountainous wilderness, surrounded by the sound of the gurgling spring and its landscape of pastel colors, allowed his mind to slow down and drift into a serene period of calmness.

Over the next few days, he estimated over thirty thousand warriors would show up to help fight the Midianites and their barbaric herd of nomads. The vacant field across the spring-fed pool he now looked at would become a place filled with the Israelites' tents, livestock, and warriors. Gideon had found a particular position by the spring and the cave to set up his tent, which would allow him private moments away from the army.

Above him rose the great mountain called Gilboa. From the valley, it soared up over sixteen hundred feet. He could see purple irises spread over the mountainside. On this day, the sun sharpened the irises' color and the light green of the grass. The mountain was vibrant. After a while, Gideon dozed off, resting comfortably with the rounded log against his back.

Further down the Jezreel Valley, the Midianites had made a camp in the shadow of Givat HaMoreh, a small mountain at the north-eastern end of the Jezreel valley. Today, the city of Afula, in modern-day Israel, occupies this area.

When you look at Givat HaMoreh from the south, it appears to be out of place across the level fields of green; a brownish bulge in the ground with areas of gray rocks haphazardly exposed, surrounded by scrub trees. It is a dark and looming figure jutting out of the tranquil Jezreel Valley.

To the north was Mount Tabor, where Deborah had defeated King Jabin and where, almost forty years later, Gideon's brothers had been murdered by Zebah and Zalmunna, the kings of the Midianites.

A millennium in the future, Mount Tabor would be the site of Jesus's transfiguration. Jesus was transformed into dazzling white on this mountaintop and visited by the Israelites' two great leaders: Moses and Elijah. Afterward, God said, "This is my Son, whom I love; with Him I am well pleased" (Matt. 3:17). Mount Tabor and the surrounding area is a connection covering the many millennia of Judeo-Christian history.

The Midianites were determined to spread out from this place and destroy all that lived and grew in Israel. These warriors were muscular, red-hued, and barbaric men who had lived a turbulent life. They spent their days marauding throughout the land, attacking smaller tribes, and consuming crops. The Midianites were takers, seldom growing crops or building permanent structures. They were a force like an angry gust that only sought to destroy. When combined with the Amalekites and the other eastern tribes, their numbers of one hundred and thirty-five thousand were a dark force preparing to destroy.

Over the next two days, Israelites from all over the lands gathered. Soon, thirty-two thousand men were encamped. Gideon observed their approach as each clan arrived and set up camp. At first, the landscaped showed the clans coming, looking like approaching dots, then as they got closer, their images became clearer. As the hours continued, the dots on the horizon became more numerous and merged, becoming a singular mass marching toward the spring.

Gideon stood, somewhat overwhelmed at what had been unleashed. The arrival of these men reinforced that a mighty task for God and the Israelites had to be accomplished.

Not too long ago, Gideon had been hiding and threshing wheat in a winepress. Now, he was the leader of a great army and God's conduit for freeing the people of Israel. The youngest of the weakest clan of the weakest tribe in Israel was now the chosen emissary of God.

God Sends Away the Fearful

The morning after the Israelites had all gathered by the Spring of Harod, Gideon stooped down and went into the cave where the spring emanated. He walked, slightly hunched over, along a small rock walkway. Finally, he found a spot where, even though his back was against a cold and wet rock, he could kneel and pray. It was a prayer full of thanksgiving and a request for wisdom.

Quickly, he heard God say, "You have too many men. I cannot deliver Midian into their hands, or Israel would boast against me, 'My own strength has saved me.' Now announce to the army, anyone who trembles with fear may turn back and leave" (Judg. 7:2–3).

Gideon had by now learned that God was up to something when He advised him to do something contrary to human logic. He searched his mind for why God would make such a strange request.

From the spies who had seen the Midianites' encampment to the northeast, he knew that the Midianites and their allies numbered one hundred and thirty-five thousand. It seemed very odd for God to make this request for reduction. But Gideon was getting used to not knowing precisely what God was up to and instead just accepting God was involved. Here was another one of those moments in which his obedience was all that was required.

As Gideon thought about God's request, he was taken back to a story he had heard from the past, which would later appear in Deuteronomy 20:8 of the Jewish Bible.

Note that the formal Bible had not yet been written during Gideon's time. The entire text of the Jewish Bible would come many centuries later. Until then, most of the stories that would later appear in the Bible were orally transmitted.

This story was of Gideon's ancestors preparing for battle during the exodus out of Egypt. The Israelites were given God's instructions on how to wage war against their enemies. God had said, "Is anyone afraid or fainthearted? Let him go home so that his fellow soldiers will not become disheartened too."

Gideon knew this was wise counsel, and maybe this was what God was up to now. He wondered how many would turn and leave. Gideon left the cave wondering what God was doing but remained steadfastly committed to following the instructions.

He held an early morning meeting, gathering up all the leaders of the various clans and tribes. The leaders stood in front, forming a half-circle around Gideon. When all had arrived, he picked up a stick from the ground, then kneeled on his right knee and braced himself with his left leg. With the stick, he drew a map on the ground showing where the Midianites were camped. Then, looking up to gauge the leaders' reactions, he told them the force in the distance numbered one hundred and thirty-five thousand.

He could see the shock in some of the leaders' faces. Eyebrows arched, and frowns appeared. This was not what they had expected. They knew it was a large and menacing force, but not this big.

Gideon went quiet for a moment to let reality set in. Then, he told them God had asked him to reduce the size of their army. Hands went up, and exasperated shrugs met this statement.

Gideon explained it was God's command so that all would know it was God who won a great battle. Gideon reminded them of the well-known story, which would later appear in Deuteronomy 20. Throughout the crowd, a steady murmur of complaint could be heard.

Then the leaders asked how and how many? Gideon said he wasn't sure how many God wanted to leave, but God had told him to allow those who were fearful to go home.

Many of the leaders were stunned at such an odd request. However, some stayed quiet and, in their minds, reconciled that this was a matter of faith in God.

The doubting leaders, of which there were many, complained to Gideon about God's bizarre request. Those were the leaders who, while somewhat committed to Gideon, were still using their human reasoning. Logic told them the force they were going to contend with was very large, and indeed, they needed every man.

Gideon vigorously stressed that this was a request from God and reminded them that God's power, not human effort, determines success.

The clan leaders knew Gideon had been receiving direction from God. But many were still not ready to give up their convictions. So, reluctantly, many of the leaders went back and held similar meetings throughout the camp.

Throughout the day, the men had many discussions. Some gathered in small groups, while others had quiet one-on-one exchanges. These smaller, intimate discussions went on throughout the camp. Gideon sat quietly by the cave, watching the men talk. Some conversations were vigorous, with arms waving to make a point. Others just knelt and spoke quietly with each other.

At first, a few left. As the day wore on, the warriors with strong doubts, seeing others leave, likewise gave in and left. By noon, a steady stream began to leave. And on it went throughout the afternoon.

Those leaving had begun to rationalize that their army was too small and they would be doomed. Others had been hesitant to come and came only because other members of their town did. And still others knew firsthand of the savagery of their foe.

By dusk, the steady stream had dwindled, and by evening it had stopped. Twenty-two thousand warriors left that day. All that was left in the camp that night were ten thousand brave and faithful warriors. Gideon's army was now outnumbered thirteen to one.

That night, Gideon was restless. He knew God was up to something, and he couldn't still his mind enough to sleep. He knew the wisdom of the verse in Deuteronomy. Having too many fearful men would erode the faith of those who remained. He also understood that God wanted to show that He would provide salvation for the people of Israel Himself, much like He had done at the great crossing of the Red Sea centuries earlier during the exodus out of Egypt.

Still, this was a lot for Gideon to absorb. Tossed, not by a lack of faith in God but more by the strangeness of this latest request, Gideon got little sleep.

When the sky lightened and the day was about to begin, Gideon went back into the cave to pray. This was a quiet time when the camp was still, and few men were up. In an hour or so, the camp would come alive with the men making breakfast. A droning buzz would fill the air, and there would be a steady activity with the army getting ready to start the day.

For Gideon, these early mornings in the cave were a peaceful time that he spent in prayer and reflection. Even as a young teen, he had learned to cherish this time. In the evening, he looked forward to when his eyes opened from sleep the following morning.

Whenever Gideon prayed, a gentle spirit would come over him. Warmth and joy filled his being. It was his time alone with God. Before his recent visits from God, it was a different time of peace—a time the Spirit would help him mold his thoughts. During these periods, he would cleanse his mind and plan his day.

The Ten Thousand are Reduced to Three Hundred

This morning was different. It was a more significant moment than in the past. Gideon knew the fate of his nation was to be determined. So, as he quieted his mind, he asked God, "What do you have for me today, Lord."

Once again, God responded and said to Gideon, "There are still too many men. Take them down to the water, and I will thin them out for you there. If I say, 'This one shall go with you,' he shall go; but if I say, 'This one shall not go with you,' he shall not go" (Judg. 7:4).

Once again, Gideon was amazed and somewhat startled by this new request. Yesterday, he watched as the numbers in his army had dramatically shrunk, now it appeared it would get even smaller. God wanted to chisel down the army and make the human task of saving a nation even harder.

As Gideon emerged from the cave, he noticed the camp's activity. Men were finishing up their breakfast and getting ready to assemble to hear the instructions for the day—all brave men looking to help. While this group numbered much smaller than yesterday, they were braver.

Gideon gathered the leaders together for the morning meeting. He delivered the news that God wanted the group even smaller. Again, Gideon saw the leaders looking at each other to gauge everyone's reaction to this startling revelation.

Each person who heard the news was shocked. They, too, wondered what God was up to with this new request. The acrimony from yesterday's announcement didn't persist, just raw surprise.

Gideon told the leaders to take their men to the pool, one group at a time. He wanted the men to go to the pool and drink from it. The message went out throughout the camp. Each clan would go, one at a time, and drink at the pool. Gideon would sit alone on a rock outcrop and watch throughout the day.

Obediently, the leaders began leading their clans to the pool by the spring. As Gideon was sitting on the rock outcrop, he heard God say, "Separate those who lap the water with their tongues as a dog laps from those who kneel down to drink" (Judg. 7:5).

On the outcrop, Gideon intensely observed how each man drank. A few bent down quickly, reached into the water with cupped hands, rose, and lapped the water from their hands. Gideon noticed these men would stay alert to their surroundings while drinking. These men were able to lap the water in their cupped hands and still look around with their eyes darting back and forth. They were alert and ready. Gideon sent these men to a nearby oak tree, where they could sit in the shade, protected by the flowing branches congested with leaves.

As each person was sent to the oak tree, there were welcoming nods from those already there. They alertly watched the process throughout the day. As the small group grew larger, they developed theories about why they were separated and discussed them amongst themselves. Back and forth, they talked, dismissing some ideas and pondering others. A quiet nervousness settled upon the group. Finally, three hundred men stood under the oak tree at the end of the afternoon. At the end of this lengthy exercise, the three hundred wondered if they had done something right or something wrong?

Most of the other men knelt and put their mouths in the water to drink, focused only on sipping the water. These men Gideon sent back to the camp.

By late afternoon, the final clan had drunk from the spring. Most men were sent back to camp. The three hundred, who lapped the water from cupped hands, were separated under and around the oak tree. There was significant discussion amongst these men, not knowing what it meant to be separated or sent back. Some assumed those who'd lapped the water would be sent home. Others wondered what this had to do with getting ready to fight the Midianites. What Gideon and God were up to was the question on everyone's mind.

As the day ended, Gideon sat alone on the outcrop. He wondered throughout the day, *Why this exercise?* Then it occurred to Gideon why God wanted him to select those who cupped the water and lapped. They were those who stayed aware of their surroundings even when drinking. God wanted warriors who would be alert at all times and ready to act in an instant.

When the men had dipped and cupped their hands, they looked around as well—never taking their eyes off their surroundings. These men were the alert and ready observers.

Gideon wasn't sure why being especially alert would help three hundred men fight one hundred and thirty-five thousand. He still wondered what God's plan was.

It seemed to Gideon that God was reading his mind as he sat on the rock outcrop because God spoke and said, "With the three hundred men that lapped, I will save you and give the Midianites into your hands. Let all the others go home" (Judg. 7:7).

Gideon took a deep breath and tried to comprehend how three hundred brave and alert warriors would save Israel. He knew they were faithful men. Their private faithfulness had become the prerequisite for this very public role God had assigned them.

Searching for the logic of this new command from God, Gideon could not understand where this would lead. He knew that God had put all thirty-two thousand men through two tests: one to find those who were the bravest and most faithful, the second, to see who would stay alert and ready. He continued to think, *What is God up to?*

He had seen God leave dew on a fleece. He watched the angel of the Lord disintegrate an offering. Gideon had experienced God saving him from the angry townspeople. He certainly knew of the great history of God rescuing his people. But now, he, an ordinary man, must obey an even more audacious request: fight one hundred and thirty-five thousand barbarians with three hundred men. Struggling with his human fears, Gideon walked back to camp.

He told those who had been sent back to the camp, "Thank you for coming. God only needs the three hundred who stand under the oak tree." Incredulous, they all left the camp wondering how this tiny army would win any battle. At Gideon's request, they left the torches, clay pots, and trumpets.

Now the three hundred knew they were staying—a small band to fight a vast horde of dangerous and wild men. They would be the ones God would use to save a nation.

Faith Questions to Discuss

1. What was God looking for in the three hundred He selected to fight? Would God find the same in you?

2. When do you encounter God in your life? Are your experiences similar to Gideon's?

3. Why is your faithfulness important to God?

4. Gideon knew it was more important to know that God was involved than to know God's final plan. What do you have to let go of to achieve this state of mind?

7

Gideon Invades the Midianite Camp

Gideon had dinner with the three hundred without much explanation for the sudden loss in the size of the army. After dinner, he went back to his tent with his mind absorbed in trying to understand what God was asking of him. Gideon needed some time to digest the events of that day. He knew God had a plan, and he faithfully believed God had not led him to the Spring of Harod to die.

Gideon felt he knew why God had picked the men. They were brave, faithful men and ever alert. They would not run away in fear and would always be watchful, never surprised. It was a good group that could be trusted on all occasions. But how did God want this tiny band to attack and defeat the Midianites?

Gideon's mind would not rest from wondering what was next. His many thoughts needed to be organized and evaluated, sorting out what was either fearful thinking or clear-headed. With no answers developed, Gideon rose to his knees from his mat and prayed for clarity.

Soothed from praying, Gideon felt his mind slow down, and he fell asleep. After an hour, he was awakened and sat straight up. He had been aroused by God, who said, "Get up; go down against the camp because I am going to give it into your hands. If you are afraid to attack, go down to the camp with your servant

Purah and listen to what they are saying. Afterward, you will be encouraged to attack the camp" (Judg. 7:9–11).

Gideon had now become used to these strange directions from God. He obediently got up, roused Purah, and told him all he had just heard from God. Together they immediately went down to the camp.

Purah, a humble and quiet person, had come to work on Gideon's father's farm a few years earlier. He had always been an encouraging voice for Gideon. Gideon liked working with Purah on various projects and tasks around the farm. Purah kept his tasks in front of him, never complaining or getting angry. He liked working with Gideon, who was non-judgmental and always open to his thoughts on how to proceed.

Like Gideon, Purah loved God and felt comfortable talking with Gideon about the ways of God. Over time they had grown close. Purah especially liked talking with Gideon because there was no hidden agenda to work around. Gideon always heard him out, and Purah would notice a softening on Gideon's face when Gideon agreed with his point of view. Purah trusted God before his own thoughts. He knew God saw more than he did. As a result, Purah became a reliable worker and faith-filled confidant for Gideon.

Now he was going on this journey with Gideon, unsure where it would lead. Purah knew Gideon and his faith in God. He also knew Gideon's name meant "great destroyer." He would gladly follow.

Purah lived precisely as his name implies: "to bear fruit." When Gideon had a difficult task, it was Purah he selected. God knew Purah was just what Gideon needed to move forward at this moment.

Once again, God was patient with Gideon as Gideon pondered his next steps in being faithful. In turn, Gideon knew God would not send him to a dangerous place without the right resources.

Purah and Gideon Spy on the Midianite Camp

Gideon and Purah left the camp and began the journey across the valley of Jezreel to hear what God said would give them confidence. They walked quietly and carefully. Sometimes they stopped to listen for anything moving. Alone in the early evening, they walked through grass that was just a little above their ankles. The dew-filled grass wet their feet.

Soon they were at the top of a dip in the valley and arrived at a spot, where just below, the Midianites camp stretched out before them. They hid behind scrub pine bushes to observe all they saw.

It was the first time Gideon had seen the camp. He had heard about it from the spies he sent, but seeing it firsthand, Gideon was utterly amazed at its size. Stretching out before him, Gideon saw lights from the campfires that seemed to expand throughout the valley. He saw camels—far too many to count. An incredible landscape of lights, warriors, and livestock spanned out before him.

Gideon and Purah crept down the dip from bush to bush using the scrub pine cover. Patiently, they moved closer to the outpost of the camp. When they arrived at the first sentry outpost, they stopped. They were now close enough to hear what was being said and remain unseen.

Shortly after, they heard one of the sentry's telling another sentry about an unsettling dream he had the night before. Then the sentry described the dream by saying, "A round loaf of barley bread came tumbling into camp. It struck the tent with such force that the tent overturned and collapsed" (Judg. 7:13).

Alarmed, the other sentry said, "This can be nothing other than the sword of Gideon, Son of Joash, the Israelite. God has given the Midianites and the whole camp into his hands" (Judg. 7:14).

Gideon and Purah backed away. Careful not to make any rustling, they moved out to a place where they could discuss what they had just heard without being noticed by the guards.

Purah, in barely a whisper, spoke first. "Remarkably, they know all about you and your conversations with God. They know you are a threat and that God will deliver victory to us."

Purah had spoken confidently. His interpretation of the dream and the other guard's confirmation gave Gideon confidence. Gideon had thought the same thing as Purah. Just as God had promised, they would hear a voice that would provide them with confidence.

One thing in the sentries' conversation Gideon found quite remarkable was that the Midianites knew of him. As he reviewed the events of the past weeks, he couldn't fathom how the Midianites could know about him. This perplexed Gideon, but he moved on thinking about the barley bread toppling the tent.

At first, one might think this reference to bread meant little. However, Purah knew that barley bread was the poorest of all bread, used to feed livestock or the very poor. So, that this lowest of all food could topple a tent was important. And more specifically, a *Midianite* tent. Purah knew their small army led by Gideon (the least of all Israelites) was the barley bread, and the tent represented the entire Midianite army.

When Gideon heard the Midianite sentry telling the story, this was his first thought as well. Gideon was relieved when he heard Purah had the same opinion. Gideon now knew his mind wasn't tricking him. He wasn't being delusional or egotistical. What God told him would happen had occurred and just the way God said.

Gideon Receives God's Plan

Gideon and Purah continued crawling up to the top of the ridge to ensure they were safely away from the enemy's encampment. While Purah stood watch, Gideon fell to his knees, thanking and praising God. Gideon was confident, though still not sure how they would attack. Nevertheless, he knew once again God was involved and in control.

Much had happened since the meeting with the strange angel back at Gideon's family compound. Gideon had seen how God was working with him. His early hopefulness and testing of God were now replaced with complete confidence. Gideon was no longer surprised by these strange events.

This was God who was answering and helping him. There had been too many of these profoundly personal events that Gideon knew were meant for him and directly from God. Over the past few weeks, he had moved from being a hopeful observer of God to a knowing observer of God. As he and Purah started back, Gideon kept thinking, *I know it was you, God.*

While Gideon walked back to camp, he excitedly began to pray for God to give him the attack plan. His confidence was high, and surreal thoughts entered his mind. He knew that a head-on attack wouldn't work. Instead, he felt God wanted him to conquer the unruly band with stealth and deception. He also knew God would feed his mind with what he should do.

He wondered a little about what God would do to help, but through his faith, he knew it would come. As he walked, his strides became longer, and he stood taller. He felt God giving him the plan. As he walked, the plan became more explicit until, finally, it was firm in his mind.

They would attack with deception at night—that very night. They would encircle the Midianites and, through sight and sound, appear to be a vast army.

Then Gideon recalled the sentry's statement regarding his fear of Gideon. God had somehow fed the Midianites knowledge of Gideon and his mission. In doing this, God had raised doubt and created fear of Gideon in the minds of the Midianite army. The accomplishments of the past few weeks weren't enough to cause this concern; God had compelled the fear to exist with the Midianites.

Gideon and the Three Hundred Attack!

When Gideon arrived back at the camp, he yelled, "Get up!" The three hundred arose and sleepily went over to where Gideon and Purah stood.

Gideon told the three hundred it was time to attack. He told them about the dream and the visit to the Midianite camp. As he spoke, the three hundred could feel Gideon's confidence. They, too, became confident and encouraged.

He broke the men into bands of three, one hundred each. He and Purah handed each man a trumpet and a clay container with a torch inside.

Gideon told the group they would surround the Midianite camp that very night. He emphatically told them they must stay alert and follow his commands without pause. Exact compliance with the timing was critical to executing the plan. He also reassured them that through their combined faith, God would help them prevail.

Gideon then instructed them to watch him closely when they arrived at the edge of the camp: "When I and all who are with me light our torches and blow our trumpets, then from all around the camp do the same and shout, 'For the Lord and for Gideon'" (Judg. 7:18).

There it was, the plan. The three hundred Israelites would encircle the Midianites and give the appearance of a much larger army. Not only that, they would attempt this wildly audacious act at night—a time when few armies would consider attacking.

This plan rested entirely on guile and exact precision. Typically, a battalion was made up of one thousand soldiers, with one person assigned as the trumpeter or horn-blower. He was essentially the messenger or signal sender to the battalion. The trumpeter would stand next to the commander and use preset signals to communicate the commander's instructions.

In the days before radios and walkie-talkies, this was how armies communicated. Trumpets were also commonly used for religious events and army signals in Gideon's time.

God had inspired Gideon to use blaring trumpets, which would give the Midianites the impression they were under attack by *three hundred thousand* men—an army much larger than that of the Midianites. The key to the plan was extraordinary execution and timing; it would require brave and alert warriors.

Gideon also received inspiration for using and waving torches. In antiquity, armies rarely attacked at night, and only then with torches to help with the attack. The appearance of torches, screaming men, clay pots being broken, and horns blaring would give an army settled in a valley a horrifying and confusing sight.

At first, the three hundred were confused. But as Gideon explained the plan, knowing smiles appeared on their faces. Slowly, as it sank in, they realized this might work!

One of the men asked Gideon, "Once we have them awake and fearful, how will we attack them?"

Gideon replied, "Stay faith-filled; God will help us with that part of the plan."

God had given Gideon a plan of disguise and ingenuity. All that was required was brave and alert men. The plan was set, and the three hundred were prepared.

In the darkness, they left silently and without fear. Ever alert, they remained focused on stealth and watching for Gideon's orders.

Each of these men, picked by God, believed in Gideon. The army was confident, and they had a God-inspired plan.

In Gideon, the three hundred saw what many had not seen, especially in Gideon's youth: a man with an enduring faith. They saw a man who didn't speak often, and when he did, they knew from his respectful manner that every word was meant without harm and not ego-driven.

It was a silent walk, with each person resolute in their mission. All were sure they were being led by a great man and God.

Gideon and his band arrived at the top of the dip in the valley just before the Midianites' middle watch arrived to take over from the first watch.

In ancient times, there were three watches for military encampments. The first watch was from sunset to 10:00 p.m. The second was from 10:00 p.m. to 2:00 a.m., and the third was from 2:00 a.m. until sunrise. Gideon and the three hundred arrived just before 10:00 p.m.

The three hundred spread out encircling the camp. Gideon then told the men next to him, "Blow the trumpet, break the jar, and light the torch as soon as the guards change." Then the instructions were quietly passed on from both the right and left.

Three hundred men were now arranged uniformly around the Midianite camp, high on a hill overlooking the valley. Gideon sat and watched for the guards to change. Every man was ready for the signal and poised to do their part.

When Gideon saw the guards change, he blew his trumpet, broke his jar, and lit his torch. The other hundred in his band quickly followed. Upon seeing this, the other two bands of a hundred did the same. Then, with trumpets blaring, pottery breaking, and the torches lit, they screamed, "A sword for the Lord and for Gideon!"

Each man held his position with the torches raised in their left hands. They continued blowing the trumpets in their right hand and waved their torches vigorously with the left. The Midianites heard the commotion and came out of their tents to see and hear these mighty sights and sounds.

When the Midianites looked all around them, it seemed a vast army was attacking. They wondered if this was Gideon and his army; the stories they had heard about Gideon raised their fear.

With torchlights flickering in every direction and trumpets blowing around them, it appeared to the Midianites their vast army was doomed. Groggy from sleep and startled, they felt overwhelmed and staggered in confusion. Many wondered how such a large army could have stealthily gotten so close without being seen.

They were a beaten army, even without a sword being drawn. The men started running in every direction, terrified. They cried out for their leaders to tell them what to do but heard nothing back. Like most bullies, their leaders cowered in fear when attacked, unable to command their army.

Many of the barbarians had been newly recruited and had become confused in all the chaos. Unsure of who was friend or ally, they began to attack one another. God had caused the Midianites, Amalekites, and other eastern tribes to turn on each other. It seemed that the new recruits didn't add strength; instead, they added confusion.

Sensing the battle was lost, the leaders and some of the army fled in terror, looking for any escape route they could find. Some, led by the two kings and two princes, escaped out into the dark, but most died by the swords of their compatriots. The once-powerful army had shrunk considerably.

As the three hundred witnessed the mayhem, their confidence grew, making them blow the trumpets louder and louder and wave the torches even more vigorously. They held steady in their positions, excitedly waiting for Gideon to give them direction.

Faith Questions to Discuss

1. Gideon's prayer life is central to who he is. How are you similar or dissimilar to Gideon in this way?

2. Why does God use unusual solutions to answer our prayers?

3. Why was it essential for the men to be faith-filled to execute God's plan?

8

The Midianites Flee

As Gideon watched some of the Midianite army flee, he passed along word to stay calm and wait until all had subsided in the enemy's camp. Proceeding too early would have unveiled the ruse.

After an hour, all was calm, and what was once a mighty enemy stronghold now contained countless dead bodies. The only sign of life was the livestock left behind. Gideon instructed the three hundred to move slowly while investigating the abandoned camp, careful not to get caught in a trap.

The three hundred started on the outskirts and then moved to the center. All around them, embers smoldered in the fire pits. On the ground, men laid in the contorted positions brought on by painful deaths. The scene seemed surreal in the gloom of darkness, with dead bodies, rising smoke, and animals roaming.

The camp was stark and eerily empty. As Gideon surveyed the scene, he knew that, for the moment, the danger had passed. Yet, he did not find the princes and kings among the dead.

Disappointed, Gideon realized there was more to do. Another lesson from God: Evil is hard to destroy. To completely follow God's plan, Gideon knew he couldn't quit. He must continue to fully obey God's plan.

In the eerie gloom, some had fled and would gather up in another place. They were still a threat to the Israelites. The Midianite army, now much smaller in size, needed to be attacked again—and soon. It was time for the Israelites to be rid of the Midianites forever and finally live in peace.

Gideon suspected the remnants of the army would cross the Jordan River to recover. Crossing the Jordan, outside of the Israelite's territory, would provide the Midianites safety. This would give them a chance to regroup and pose a threat in the future. Preventing them from crossing would end the threat forever.

Gideon sent messengers throughout the land to recruit help in chasing down the fleeing enemy. He sent word to the Naphtali tribe. Naphtali was the sixth son of Jacob and leader of one of the twelve tribes of Israel. When the messengers arrived, the Naphtali people were shocked that three hundred men had defeated such a large army. As the story of Gideon's ingenuity in attacking the Midianites was told, they became believers; even the doubters were won over.

The messengers said Gideon wanted them to pursue the Midianites. The Naphtali were known for their speed, an inheritance they received from their ancestor. Quickly, the men of Naphtali went after the Midianites.

A second group of messengers went to the tribe of Asher. Asher was Jacob's eighth son and also one of the founders of the twelve original tribes of Israel. The people of Asher were known to be the mediators amongst the twelve tribes. It was a tribe filled with logical and truthful people, much like their namesake. They also heard the call and were amazed at Gideon's great victory. Soon they, too, were in pursuit of the Midianites.

All of Manasseh—Gideon's tribe—were told of the victory, and the messengers requested they pursue the Midianites, emboldened because they knew of Gideon first-hand as a member of their tribe. They joined as well.

Gideon also needed a group to stand by the Jordan River to prevent a crossing. He knew the best place for the fleeing army to cross the Jordan would be at Beth Barah, where the Jordan was more expansive and tamer. For centuries, it was a customary place to cross.

Reluctantly, Gideon sent messengers to the tribe of Ephraim, closest to where the Midianites would cross the Jordan River at Beth Barah, or "a place to ford" in English. He knew they would be haughty and upset that they were omitted from Gideon's earlier plan. They were a proud tribe, and Gideon needed them now. He would smooth any discord later. But for this moment, they were necessary to prevent the Midianites from crossing the Jordan and regrouping.

Through messengers, the tribe of Ephraim was asked to guard the Jordan river as far as Beth Barah, further south of Beth Shittah. For the people of Ephraim, their short easterly journey would be aided by a gap in the mountains. It was a valley that ran to the east and would lead them directly to Beth Barah.

In his message to Ephraim, Gideon said, "Come down against the Midianites and seize the waters of the Jordan ahead of them as far as Beth Barah" (Judg. 7:24).

Though still upset about being left out of Gideon's plans, the men of Ephraim complied and spread out along the west side of the Jordan River. Some went into positions high in the mountains, which lined the river in spots. Others laid in wait amongst fifteen-foot-tall reeds.

From these positions, they could watch the Midianites move south to Beth Barah. Then, after the Midianites passed, they would follow the Midianites stealthily, monitoring their progress toward the fording place.

The Midianites Surprising Division

The Midianites were unaware of the Israelites' plan. Their sole focus was to escape and find a secure place while they figured out their next steps.

As the Midianites continued south along the western shore of the Jordan River toward Beth Barah, they unexpectedly found another place to cross. While this place would not be as easy as the crossing at Beth Barah, it seemed possible. The Kings, Zebah and Zalmunna, stated they would cross here. Their sons, Oreb and Zeeb, disagreed. A lengthy and acrimonious debate occurred.

Zebah and Zalmunna wanted to get to safety quickly and thought that the faster they could get into the mountains, the better off they would be. In their minds, the added danger of crossing here and not at Beth Barah was offset by the speed of being out of Israelite territory.

Oreb and Zeeb believed that crossing the Jordan River at this point, while shorter, was far riskier. They had also become wary of their fathers' ability to lead after the Jezreel Valley disaster. Many men in the army also had begun to whisper amongst themselves, embarrassed by the defeat. The kings had lost control; no longer did their fear tactics work on some in their army.

Seeing a chance to usurp the kings and become the leaders, Oreb and Zeeb insisted they continue to Beth Barah. While half in the army had doubts, others—fifteen thousand—remained loyal to the kings. There would be no reconciliation. The kings and fifteen thousand crossed the river. The princes chose to take the remainder of the army south to Beth Barah for a safer crossing.

Zebah and Zalmunna would try to cross the Jordan and travel to where it met up with the Jabbok River. They would then follow the Jabbok to a mountain pass and head south to Karkor.

Getting to safety was the kings' primary concern. Once they got to their hiding place, they could regroup and ponder their subsequent movements. Only the tribe of Gad, named after the seventh son of Jacob, would stand in the way of the kings' journey to freedom.

While Gad was part of the twelve tribes of Israel, some of the Israelites viewed the people of Gad as inferior because of questionable ancestry. Some of the Israelites thought that Zilpah, Gad's mother and Jacob's third wife, was only a handmaiden and not worthy of being the matriarch of a tribe of Israel. In fact, Gad in Hebrew means "luck," and some felt it was only through luck that they were included as a tribe of Israel.

A short distance east of Gad was the land of Ammon. Here the Midianite kings could regroup and try again to attack the Israelites or vanish into the wilderness to resume their old lives.

The two princes went their own way, having lost faith and trust in the kings. Any decision the kings would make, they now doubted. Filled with pride, they thought they could have done better in the Jezreel Valley.

After years of listening, the two princes now wanted to decide the course of events and be in charge. With the defeat, any counsel the kings gave them was met with suspicion and defiance. In their minds, it was their time, and the princes thought they knew best.

For the kings and their sons, dividing up the army would prove to be a disastrous decision.

The Battle at Beth Barah

The Ephraim scouts who had seen this division quickly headed to the south to tell their leaders what had happened. This wasn't what anyone had suspected, and now their foe was divided.

The leaders of Ephraim saw this as good and bad—good that they would fight a weakened enemy, bad that they would lose their chance to be the ones who ultimately ended the savage reign of the Midianites.

The unsuspecting group led by the haughty and defiant Oreb and Zeeb headed south to Beth Barah. The two princes were excited; now they were in charge, and things would be different. Feeling elated and sure of themselves, they relished their freedom and ability to decide what would happen next.

Gideon thought the Midianites would turn south when they arrived at Beth Shittah, which is what happened. Going north led to the Sea of Galilee and would offer them little protection and only move them deeper into the land of the Israelites. Going south was the only logical direction.

This path would put them on the west side of the Jordan River. When they arrived at Beth Barah, they could cross the Jordan River. There, they could either climb the rugged and challenging mountains that bordered the Jordan River or turn north.

This northerly turn would be far more accessible and take them to a valley created by the Jabbok River to avoid the mountains' strenuous climb. In theory, this sounded good. However, Gideon had not predicted the division that occurred.

The tale of the three hundred quickly spread through the land while the Midianite army was escaping. The Israelites now had hope—God had heard their cries. Even the tribe of Ephraim had become willing to help. Those doubtful became believers. Those previously afraid became brave. The Israelites were now a united nation.

Weakened from the Jezreel Valley's chaos, the princes' army was tired from traveling along the Jordan to Beth Barah. The once-powerful army was now a much smaller and a divided remnant.

The men of Ephraim, hidden in reeds and behind trees in the mountains that lined the riverbank, watched the Midianites, led by the princes, arrive at the place to ford.

When the divided Midianite band arrived at Beth Barah, they thought perhaps they had been right. This crossing looked much more effortless than where the kings were trying to cross upriver. But as the princes watched their men congregate to prepare for the crossing, disaster came in the form of screaming men who encircled them.

Rising from the reeds and behind the trees, the men of Ephraim attacked. The Midianites became utterly disoriented. The princes and their band quickly succumbed to the men of Ephraim.

The battle didn't last long; the chased were quickly overwhelmed by the guards at their only escape route. This group of Midianites who had come to pillage and destroy now did not have enough to put up a fight against the men of Ephraim—a people who saw a chance to be released from seven years of fear.

The men of Ephraim found and killed the two princes. Oreb was killed by a rock outcrop, which today is called the Rock of Oreb or Orbo. Zeeb was found hiding in a winepress and killed. It is ironic that Zeeb, a leader of the Midianites, was killed in a winepress similar to the one Gideon had stealthily labored many mornings—a subtle but important message from God.

Ephraim's men cut off the princes' heads as proof of their great victory and a way to prove their greatness to Gideon.

Soon after, Gideon and the three hundred arrived at Beth Barah. Ephraim's leaders laid the two princes' heads before Gideon. It was both a gesture of proof and a veiled way of saying to Gideon, "You should have involved us earlier."

Faith Questions to Discuss

1. In staying patient, Gideon allowed God's plan to unfurl. Has there been a time in your life when more patience would have helped you with God's answer to your prayers?

2. Why did the Israelites feel more hopeful as God's plan began to take shape? Have there been examples of this in your own life?

3. Have you experienced disappointment in executing God's plan? How did you react?

4. What is the irony of Zeeb, the prince, being discovered in a winepress? Is God using irony to send a message?

9

The People of Sukkoth Deny Gideon

Gideon sat alone by the Jordan River. It had been a few days since he had been able to rest and think through the events of the great but partial victory in the valley of Jezreel. Gideon needed a few moments alone.

He was thankful that the men of Ephraim had won their battle and prevented a large group of Midianites from escaping over the river. However, he also knew the Midianite's army, reduced to perhaps fifteen thousand strong, remained. Led by the two kings, Zebah and Zalmunna, the remnants of the Midianites were still out there roaming and looking for an escape. If they found one, they could rise again in some distant future to invade Israel. Gideon thought to himself, *Evil is a persistent foe.*

Gideon and the three hundred needed rest. And Gideon had to soothe the Ephraim tribe, who felt left out. As with any great victory, there are always those who feel slighted.

After a brief rest and reflection, Gideon approached the Ephraim leaders to hear their complaints. Gideon knew that many more Midianites would have escaped without them, and they deserved recognition. Always careful to be humble, Gideon approached the leaders and thanked them.

In return, they said to Gideon, "Why have you treated us like this? Why didn't you call us when you went to fight Midian?" (Judg. 8:1). This was a tricky question to answer.

Gideon knew God's instructions for selecting the three hundred were rigorous and eliminated many from fighting in the Jezreel Valley. However, Gideon didn't pass the blame onto God. Instead, he explained why the plan worked. It became apparent the selection of the three hundred from over thirty-two thousand and not asking the Ephraim people to help had ruffled the tribe, not just slightly but very intensely. They vigorously challenged Gideon to give them a better answer.

Gideon realized that Oreb and Zeeb's deaths were mighty accomplishments and had severely limited the Midianites' abilities. The Ephraim people had crippled the escaping Midianites, and Gideon was grateful.

Gideon asked Ephraim's leaders, "What have I accomplished compared to you? Aren't the gleanings of Ephraim's grapes better than the full grape harvest of Abiezer? God gave Oreb and Zeeb, the Midianite leaders, into your hands. What was I able to do compared to you?" (Judg. 8:2–3).

Through this humble question, Gideon spoke words that soothed Ephraim's people. For so long, Ephraim had grown used to having leaders who tried to exalt themselves instead of praising God and those who helped.

They talked a bit longer about the previous battles, with Gideon explaining everything he had experienced with God. In Gideon, they found a committed leader who thought of unity and not personal gain—an unusual trait not seen in a leader for many decades.

Likewise, with the other tribes, they had heard the stories of Gideon and his following God faithfully. They had also heard about his humble fairness. The Israelites now knew Gideon never sought his own glory; he only sought God's ways to help the people of Israel.

The Leaders of Sukkoth Deny Gideon

Gideon knew the logical route for the two kings and the remaining Midianites would be to head east, up the Jabbok River Valley near where they had crossed, then travel toward Karkor. He sent messengers to tell the tribes of Naphtali, Manasseh, and Asher to meet him in Sukkoth.

Gideon also asked the warriors of Ephraim to join him in this final attack. He went with his three hundred and the men of Ephraim to Sukkoth to seek rest. In crossing the Jordan River easterly, Gideon entered the tribal territory of Gad—the land where the town of Sukkoth existed.

Gad was one of two Israelite tribes that lived east of the Jordan and outside the Promised Land on the western side of the Jordan River. Centuries earlier, Moses had reluctantly permitted the tribes of Gad and Reuben to reside in this eastern territory.

Before the crossing of the Jordan River after the forty-year exodus from Egypt, the leaders of the Gad tribe asked Moses if they could settle on the eastern side of the Jordan. The tribe of Gad had numerous sheep. The region on the eastern side of the Jordan River had open and fertile valleys, which would provide the tribe with better grazing fields than any area west of the Jordan.

At first, Moses refused this request. He thought the tribes that did not enter the Promised Land would not help eliminate the pagan tribes and become alienated.

The leaders of Gad vigorously appealed this decision. They assured Moses they would go to the other side of the Jordan and help tame the land. Moses reluctantly gave in to their request.

After Joshua led the twelve tribes over the Jordan, the tribe of Gad was granted this land. Moses did not enter the Promised Land and died on top of Mount Nebo, in the territory of Gad.

Many centuries in the future, an ominous event would occur because Gad's leaders were always too political. Their leaders were cagey people, frequently searching for what was in their best interest. It seemed Moses may have been right. Allowing them to separate from the other tribes reduced their loyalties to their nation.

The two kings and their divided army successfully crossed north of Beth Barah. Now they were focused on moving into the mountains to gather up and rest.

Sukkoth was on the way to Karkor, where Gideon assumed the remaining Midianites and two kings would pass. Gideon would go east across the Jordan, then north along the river. He would head east at the Jabbok River Valley that contained the towns of Sukkoth and Peniel. In Sukkoth, they would rest and recover before heading on to deal with the Midianites.

Jacob founded Sukkoth many centuries earlier after completing a twenty-year exile. He built a house and place for cattle; he called the place Sukkoth. Interestingly, it is the exact name of one of three major annual holidays for the Israelites. It is a festival that commemorates the Israelites' sheltering during the wilderness wanderings after the exodus from Egypt. Gideon hoped Sukkoth would provide the same shelter for him and the army. This critical town along major trade routes was where the descendants of Jacob's son, Gad, had settled after the exodus from Egypt.

Many would seek refuge in this town conveniently located near the Jordan River and trade routes. When Gideon arrived, he was also seeking rest. Gideon met with the town's leaders and requested bread plus a field for his exhausted and famished troops to camp and rest. He told the leaders he was still chasing the Midianite kings and would not stay long.

Stunningly, the town leaders refused Gideon and accused him of lying. They told him, "Do you already have the hands of Zebah and Zalmunna in your possession? Why should we give bread to your troops?" (Judg. 8:6).

Even though they would benefit from the Midianites' defeat, they didn't want to get into the middle of the fight between the Midianites and Gideon. Moreover, they had seen the Midianite army of fifteen thousand men pass by earlier. They doubted Gideon would be victorious in his quest with their craftily worded question.

They saw how exhausted and famished the men with Gideon were and knew that the Midianite army was still large in number. Fearing later reprisal from the Midianites was part of the reason they refused to offer Gideon any assistance. The leaders' loyalty to Gideon was also subdued from three hundred years of feeling like outcasts by their brethren on the other side of the Jordan.

And lastly, Gideon posed a threat to their leadership in this tightly ruled community. They were jealous of Gideon's fame and feared the people of Sukkoth would become enamored with Gideon, reducing their power. The less the townspeople saw of Gideon, the better.

The leaders of Sukkoth made a grievous error out of fear and lack of trust in God—one which would cost them in the very near future. Despite all Gideon and his men had done to save the Israelites, the leaders of Sukkoth turned their backs on Gideon.

Tired from his journeys and disappointed by the treatment of the leaders of Sukkoth, Gideon blurted out, "Just for that, when the Lord has given Zebah and Zalmunna into my hand, I will tear your flesh with desert thorns and briers" (Judg. 8:7).

Gideon and the army left Sukkoth.

The Leaders of Peniel Also Deny Gideon

Not far from Sukkoth was the town of Peniel, another major outpost of the tribe of Gad. Peniel was made famous many centuries before the tribe's arrival. Here, Jacob (Israel) wrestled with a stranger in this city, whom he later recognized as God. After Jacob's mighty spiritual and physical battle with God, it was in Peniel that God changed Jacob's name to Israel. Perhaps this town would house Gideon and his men.

As Gideon approached Peniel, he eyed the city from a distance. He saw the Jabbok River flowing in the valley near the town. Vibrant green trees grew close to the river, nourishing their roots. All that grew near this river was a lush green, a harsh contrast to nearby mountains containing a near-desert yellowish-brown landscape.

As he walked along the river, red and brown boulders jutted up from the water, which revealed the low water level. It was here that many from the east would cross and visit Peniel, as would Gideon.

When he entered the city, he went to the city leaders and requested a place to stay and food for his men. Like their brethren in Sukkoth, the leaders of Peniel also turned Gideon away. They had also seen the Midianite army pass by from a very tall tower on the city's outskirts. The leaders of another town had chosen to reject Gideon because they feared the Midianites and Gideon's fame.

Most of the Israelites had heard the story of Gideon's great victories, as had the leaders of Sukkoth and Peniel. The townspeople of Sukkoth and Peniel wanted to support Gideon, but their leaders chose otherwise. Although the leaders of these two towns had much to gain by believing God was with Gideon, their fear of the Midianites and the potential effect of Gideon's fame on their power with the townspeople caused them to refuse Gideon.

As Gideon was leaving Peniel, he saw the tower that stood watch over the town. It was a narrow circular structure with just enough room for one person to climb up rough stone steps to the observation post on top. From this vantage point of one hundred feet high, travelers could be spotted crossing the Jabbok River, providing a significant advantage for the town. As Gideon was leaving, he pointed to the tower and said, "When I return in triumph, I will tear down this tower" (Judg. 8:9).

Disappointed at being rejected and still having to chase down those who sought to destroy his nation, Gideon wondered what other challenges he would face before subduing the two kings. Nevertheless, he proceeded resolutely, not letting his disappointment derail him from serving God and his nation. Disappointment would not make him compromise his mission from God.

The leaders of these two towns had acted out of selfishness. At a time when the Israelites were close to victory, the leaders of Peniel and Sukkoth chose their human desires over the ways of God. This was the same mistake the entire nation made, which caused the Midianites to invade their land seven years earlier. God is a mighty foe for those who seek personal gain.

Faith Questions to Discuss

1. The leaders of Peniel and Sukkoth chose to protect their power over the townspeople instead of helping Gideon. Why is this a flawed strategy?

2. Why were Gideon's faith and humbleness crucial in rallying the Israelites?

3. Has there been a time when you sought safety or personal gain over following God's plan?

10

The Final Battle with the Midianites

East along the Jabbok River, beyond Peniel and Sukkoth, is a narrow path leading to a broad depression in the mountains called Karkor. Gideon had suspected and now received word that the Midianites were camped there. It was a perfect hiding place for the Midianite army to rest.

The Midianites had been on the run for days and were exhausted. All that was left of their army was fifteen thousand men. One hundred and twenty thousand had died either in the Jezreel Valley or by the Jordan River at the hands of the Ephraim tribe.

The Midianites were desperately trying to find a place to rest. Zebah and Zalmunna knew things looked bleak. For the last few days, when they looked back at the horizon, they saw the dust of the people of Naphtali, Asher, Ephraim, and all the armies of Manasseh in pursuit.

This once marauding army, which had tormented the Israelites for seven years, was now the one being chased. Zebah and Zalmunna knew their only choice was to escape across the Jordan and head into the mountains. As Gideon had suspected, the Midianite army's remnants fled across the Jordan to the east. They passed the towns of Sukkoth and Peniel, whose leaders had seen the Midianites passing and became fearful.

Pressing forward, the Midianites found the pass, which took them to a hideaway in the mountains—Karkor. The Midianites headed south into the mountains. They were a tired group whose energy was fueled by the fear of being caught.

As they arrived at the top of a mountain and looked below, they saw a stream fed by the infrequent rains in the high desert below them. When they descended, they spotted a bend in the stream, which held small trees and vegetation—a suitable place to rest and hide. They had reached Karkor.

All around them were mountains the light brown color of the desert. There was little vegetation except for a few desert brushes. When it did rain, water quickly ran down the mountainsides and into the rills created by the many centuries of run-off. Nomads had crossed through here many times, forming the trails that now existed.

As they had made their way down to Karkor, the Midianites no longer saw the troops in the distance, which had been chasing them the previous days. Perhaps the Israelites had finally dropped out of the chase and went back across the Jordan. They began to feel hopeful they could rest in this desolate space. Perhaps, after a few days of rest, they would find a way out.

Gideon Follows a Different Path to the Midianites

Spies had told Gideon exactly where the Midianites were staying. Gideon chose not to follow the pass to Karkor, which the Midianites had taken. Even though the army was tired, Gideon would go a different and tougher route, one the Midianites would not suspect.

Before he left, Gideon had met up with the other Israelites near Peniel. He now had a suitable army with which to pursue the Midianites.

He was frustrated that the fight to end the evil which had invaded his land seemed to have never-ending twists. Still, he had work to finish for God and the Israelites. To turn around now would only give the Israelites a partial victory and leave Gideon knowing he had not satisfied God's will.

Gideon once again laid out his plan for the attack on the remnants of the marauders from the east. Bypassing the southerly turn into the mountains the Midianites took, the Israelites would continue on a short distance and climb a path used by nomads from the north. Then, instead of arriving from the north into Karkor, they would come from the east, where the Midianites would be completely surprised.

At dusk, after they had eaten, the Israelites filled up their water containers and began the climb over the desert mountains, led by Gideon. There would be no brownish dust to be seen at night. They would be unnoticed. The climbs were challenging, much more difficult than how the Midianites had arrived in Karkor. Fortunately, each time they crested a top, they were greeted with a short, easy decline, which refreshed their legs.

Finally, they arrived at a pass that would take them down into Karkor. The access was a well-worn path that had been used by nomads for centuries. On either side of them rose high peaks, looking like brownish-gray walls at night. It was a quiet and still place with no wind. Darkness surrounded them. With morning close, the army hurried so they could attack just before dawn.

The Final Battle

Before they descended, Gideon prayed and asked for God's blessings and protection for the Israelite army. As Gideon gave out the descent and battle instructions, he told the army not to kill Zebah and Zalmunna. Gideon had another purpose for them in Sukkoth. He wanted to capture the kings alive.

Silently, they descended toward the encampment below. In the distance, they could see the watch lights burning. Despite the many losses the Midianites had endured, stretched out in the valley, they were still a mighty army.

As Gideon had expected, the Midianites were unprepared for an attack from the nomads' path. The Midianites were utterly unsuspecting when the army roared past the outposts and into the camp.

The Midianites awoke in confusion and were unprepared to fight. They were quickly subdued. Off at the camp's far end, Gideon noticed Zebah and Zalmunna escaping. Quickly, Gideon and the three hundred pursued the kings while the other tribes of Israel engaged and fought the remaining Midianites. Soon they had encircled the two kings, who looked around and saw their routes of escape were gone.

They dismounted their camels and laid their swords on the ground. The scene seemed unreal and hard to grasp for Gideon. Just weeks ago, these kings posed a stark and potent threat to the very survival of the Israelites. Now kneeling in front of Gideon, they were defeated men.

While enormous in number, the other Midianites lacked the sense of purpose to fight and were quickly subdued. After days of being pursued and with no real noble purpose, they gave up.

Amazingly, Gideon, the youngest of Joash's sons, a member of the weakest clan, the Abiezrites, and the lowest of the twelve tribes, the Manasseh, had utterly defeated the long archenemies of the Israelites.

From a societal point of view, the lowest person in all the land was the person God picked to save the Israelites. God saw a "man of mighty valor" with a quiet strength and filled with humility. He was a brave man of great faith in God, who thought first about his tasks and ignored his desire for fame.

A Lesson for Sukkoth and Peniel

Gideon had the kings bound and headed back to Sukkoth through the Pass of Heres, just around sunup. Coincidentally,

Heres means "sun." They descended from the pass toward the Jabbok River as the glimmering sun showed over the horizon.

This route would bypass Peniel and head straight for Sukkoth. As they were traveling, they spotted a young man. When he saw the army of Israelites, he began to run but was soon overtaken and subdued. Gideon questioned him and learned he was from Sukkoth. Gideon asked the young man to tell him all the Sukkoth elders' names.

He gave Gideon seventy-seven names. Gideon knew that it wasn't the town's people that had denied them hospitality; it was the leaders.

Gideon arrived in Sukkoth with the two kings bound and tied. He asked that all the elders meet him in the center of town. No longer smug, they all gathered quickly, and Gideon said to them, "Here are the kings about whom you taunted me by saying, 'Do you already have the hands of Zebah and Zalmunna in your possession? Why should we give bread to your exhausted men?'" (Judg. 8:15).

The elders had made a wrong choice. And Gideon had brought proof of this poor decision. He had brought the captured kings they feared and now had to pay for their rejection of Gideon and God.

Gideon told the three hundred to take the elders as prisoners. Outside of town was a field of bushes heavily ladened with thorns. Parched by the sun, the thorns were dry and sharp. The elders were forced to run through the bushes. As they did, they were repeatedly scraped by the exposed thorns, enduring many cuts.

Before leaving, Gideon had warned the leaders that this would be their punishment. Gideon spared the people of Sukkoth, who, in turn, selected new leaders that would be, for a time, faithful to God.

Next, Gideon went to Peniel and likewise showed them the two kings. Peniel's elders had made a similar choice as the elders of Sukkoth. Gideon tore down the one-hundred-foot tower and banished the elders.

It was finally time to end the legacy of the Midianites. All that remained of the one hundred and thirty-five thousand marauders and bandits were the two kings, Zebah and Zalmunna.

During their initial invasion seven years earlier, the Midianites went to Mount Tabor after a major battle with the Israelites. A group of Israelites had escaped and sought refuge. The Midianites captured this band and, instead of taking them prisoners, murdered them. Two of those men were Gideon's brothers.

Gideon asked the two kings, "What kind of men did you kill at Tabor?" (Judg. 8:18).

The kings answered, "Men like you. They had the bearing of princes" (Judg. 8:18).

Gideon replied, "Those were my brothers, the sons of my own mother. As surely as the Lord lives, if you had spared their lives, I would not kill you" (Judg. 8:19).

Gideon turned to his son Jether and said, "Kill them." Gideon wanted their death to be one of disgrace, and having a boy kill them would cement their legacy. As they had ordered other men to kill his brothers, so did Gideon. Jether was a boy and trembled in fright, refusing his father's request.

The kings said to Gideon, "Come, do it yourself. As is the man, so is his strength" (Judg. 8:21). Gideon took the ornaments from around their camels' necks that had signified the kings' mighty status, then slew them. With their deaths came the death of the Midianites—not just for that day, but for all days. The brutal reign of terror throughout the land was ended entirely.

Faith Questions to Discuss

1. Was Gideon's request to have his son kill the kings an unholy act of revenge? Why are vengeful motives not aligned with God's plan?

2. What did Gideon accomplish by punishing the leaders of Sukkoth? What is the leadership lesson from their mistake?

3. How would Jesus have dealt with the two kings or the leaders of Sukkoth and Peniel?

11

Gideon Becomes the
Fifth Judge of Israel

Gideon returned to his home and his daily routines. Now he could make wine in the winepress and grind wheat in the open. Locally and nationally, he had become a celebrity, and many greeted him with praise. Gideon humbly acknowledged all that was said about him by saying, "All that I have done was for the glory of God."

Soon, Gideon was visited by the leaders of all the tribes of the Israelites. There was a cry throughout the land for him to be their king. In Gideon's father's house, the leaders met with Gideon and said, "Rule over us—you, your son, and your grandson—because you have saved us from the hand of Midian" (Judg. 8:22).

But to this request, Gideon replied, "I will not rule over you, nor will my son rule over you. The Lord will rule over you" (Judg. 8:23). Instead, Gideon became the fifth of the twelve judges that oversaw the Promised Land.

Gideon then said, "I have one request: each of you give me an earring from your share of the plunder" (Judg. 8:24).

The leaders answered, "We'll be glad to give them" (Judg. 8:25).

They placed what Gideon had requested on the purple garments worn by the two Midianite kings. When they had finished, gold equal to seventeen hundred shekels or forty-three pounds laid before Gideon.

Gideon combined this with some of the loot he had received through the Midianite kings' deaths. Gideon made an ephod with the gold and the purple garments he received during the deaths of the two kings. An ephod was a priestly garment made only for the high priests. He then placed the ephod in the center of his town, Ophrah.

Gideon made the Ephod with sincere hopes of always reminding the people of the sacredness of worshipping God. After this, people frequently came to worship the ephod. What Gideon had created innocently for good would become a false idol. Over time, the visits to Ophrah became more about seeing the great garment and less a reminder of staying faithful to God.

During Gideon's time as judge, forty years of peace came over Israel. Gideon encouraged the Israelites to continue remembering God. As a result, God looked favorably upon the Israelites.

However, the adulation and praise exposed a flaw in Gideon's character. His humility began to wane, and feelings of entitlement emerged.

While married, he took many wives. The laws of the Torah did not specifically ban polygamy for men. But polygamy was not the standard of that time. Gideon may have rationalized his behavior through the acts of previous great leaders—Moses, Jacob, and Abraham—who also had multiple wives. Through his wives, Gideon had seventy sons.

Gideon also had a concubine in Shechem, with whom he had a son named Abimelek. The name means "my father is king," precisely the role Gideon had denied assuming after the great victory over the Midianites. This last transgression would lead to disaster for the Israelites and Gideon's family in the future.

Gideon lived to an old age and, when he died, was buried in his father's tomb in Ophrah.

No sooner had Gideon died than the Israelites again stumbled and worshipped other human gods like Baal. The new generation quickly forgot the history of oppression from which Gideon had saved Israel. Guile and intrigue became the norm for society. No longer did the poor get fed. Instead, conversations of goodwill morphed into those of deception.

In Shechem, they set up Baal-Berith as their God and did not remember the Lord their God. Even more stunning, over the decades since the great battle with the Midianites, they forgot about Gideon and his bravery in defending their nation. When people forget God, they also forget their friends.

Gideon's brave lesson of overcoming evil with good and not being overcome by evil was now lost. Forgetfulness of God is often the parent of ingratitude to God. This always leads to disaster.

Abimelek plotted against Gideon's seventy sons—his own half-brothers. Desirous to be the new leader of Israel, Abimelek garnered the support of the leaders in Shechem.

Shechem was in the land of the Ephraim tribe and the capital of Israel. Its leaders were now fearful that one of Gideon's seventy sons would be the new ruler or judge. In addition, they were worried that another member of the tribe of the Manasseh would lead Israel. So, they sanctioned Abimelek to end this threat.

Abimelek hired local thugs and captured all of Gideon's sons with the support of those in Shechem. Then, one by one, Abimelek murdered each of his half-brothers on a rock in the center of Ophrah. Abimelek was crowned the ruler, but only for a short time; he would also die by a sword.

The cycle of crying out to God, being saved by God, and then turning from God continued. Who would be the next person God would use to save His people?

Faith Questions to Discuss

1. Despite God's continuous acts of salvation, why do we turn from God, only to cry out later?

2. Why did the Ephod become a false idol? What false idols do we create in our own lives?

3. Why is our forgetfulness of God "the parent of ingratitude toward God?"

4. Why did Gideon succumb to his human desires despite his faithfulness, humility, and skill as a leader?

Epilogue

After Gideon's death, the Israelites would be ruled by seven more judges. In total, twelve judges ruled over Israel for three hundred years.

For the remaining period of the judges, similar to the time before Gideon, the Israelites would experience periods of peace and faithfulness followed by periods when leaders would emerge and lead them away from God. In response, the people eventually cried out for a king, falsely thinking a king would end this wavering cycle.

Samuel, a mighty prophet who lived a century after Gideon, rose to be a wise influence on the Israelites. Despite disagreeing with the people, God helped Samuel find a king to rule Israel.

Samuel had warned the people of the dangers of kings. But the people wanted to be like their neighboring societies and insisted. Once again, the people ignored God's advice and were given a king.

Samuel met a young man named Saul, a handsome man much taller than other men. God told Samuel that Saul would be the Israelites' first king. Samuel's selection of King Saul worked well at first. However, over time Saul succumbed to the temptation of his role.

After a few disastrous events, Samuel had to look for a new king. God asked Samuel to pick the next king based on their heart and faith. The eighth and youngest son of Jesse—David—was selected. As soon as David was selected, the Spirit of the Lord left Saul, who would try many times to have David murdered.

Then in the act of resignation, before the Philistines captured him, Saul killed himself, and David became the new king. He consolidated his power and defeated the Philistines. And once again, the Israelites were saved.

King David ruled for many years. In fact, many of the Psalms were written by David. He, too, would have a few cringe-worthy moments, like having a husband of a woman he desired murdered. He also ignored the rape of his daughter Tamar by her half-brother. It seems even a person with a heart for God can fall into the grasps of temptation.

After David's death, his son Solomon rose to become king. He, too, became enamored with power. And unfortunately, after a promising start, he also became weak. David's grandson, Rehoboam, followed this reign. Then the kingship of the entire nation of the Israelites ended.

Dissatisfied and overwhelmed with the high taxes imposed by Rehoboam and his father, King Solomon, ten of the twelve tribes split from the tribes of Judah and Benjamin. The division occurred in 975 BC. The people of Israel were a divided nation. Neither judges nor kings could unite them nor keep them holy.

With this division, two new nations were formed. The ten tribes who revolted were still called the Kingdom of Israel, and Shechem remained its capital. The two tribes, Judah and Benjamin, became the Kingdom of Judah, and their capital was Jerusalem.

For another two hundred years, the new nation of Israel continued the ebb and flow between obedience and disobedience. Some kings were good, and others were disloyal to God. Finally, in 721 BC, the Assyrians took over the Kingdom of Israel. The Israelites were disbanded, and the ten tribes dissolved. These tribes today are now known as the Ten Lost Tribes of Israel.

The Kingdom of Judah, while somewhat more loyal to God, was also taken over by a foreign power. In 588 BC, Babylon's Nebuchadnezzar laid siege to Jerusalem and virtually put an end to the kingdom of Judah. Its people were taken captive into Babylon.

After seventy years in captivity, they returned to rebuild Jerusalem. However, Judah never really regained its former power. It eventually became a captured land of the Roman Empire.

Jesus, God's only Son, was sent to solve the vicious and recurring cycle of forgetting God, crying out for salvation, and then being saved. Thirty years after Jesus's arrival, he was crucified and rose on the third day. Since that first Easter, Jesus has reigned for over two thousand years.

Faith Questions to Discuss

1. Why is Jesus the answer to the ebb and flow of human faith in God?

40100569R00073